On Your Pilgrimage Called Grief

A Guide for Widows and Widowers

Bill Dodds

ISBN: 0-9840908-8-6
ISBN-13: 978-0-9840908-8-4

DEDICATION

To Eileen Putter, an extraordinarily gifted grief counselor who has been a tremendous help to so many, including me.

To the widows and widowers who were part of a spousal-loss support group sponsored by Group Health Cooperative (now Kaiser Permanente) in Redmond, Washington. (And continue to meet quarterly for a "Good Grief" potluck lunch.)

To the widows and widowers who were part of the spousal-loss support group sponsored by Providence Regional Medical Center in Everett, Washington.

I thank each and every one of you for your wisdom, advice, kindness, compassion, empathy, sharing, and listening. And—which may surprise people who are not "club members"—for so many, many times of laughter.

God bless you and the one you love so dearly.

CONTENTS

INTRODUCTION

WHERE TO BEGIN?

Where to begin when your sweetheart's life ends?

How to survive when your own will to live just wants to call it quits?

I figured I was ready for widowhood. I had even said that to a widow of more than three decades when talking to her about my wife's rapidly approaching and inevitable death from uterine cancer.

"No one is ready," she had said. I let that go but thought *I am.*

At eight o'clock in the evening of January 6, 2013, I learned I was wrong. Dead wrong. I had known little or nothing about losing a spouse and in that instant learned more than I ever wanted to know.

Since that moment my education has continued.

Widowhood is always a "crash course." But you already know that if your husband or wife has passed away. You're now a member of a club that no one wants to join because the entrance requirements are way too high. At many times and in many ways, seemingly impossible.

I Wish We Could Visit

If I had my way you and I would just sit down and visit. You could tell me some of your story and I could tell you some of mine. You could tell me what's going on with you now, today, this moment, and I could tell you what it was like for others and me when we were where you are.

One week "out." Two weeks. A month. Two months. A year. Two years. Not that we fellow widows and widowers have "the answer" but we do have what we tried. What worked for us and what didn't. How we made it from one week to two. One month to two. One year to two.

We're no experts except, of course and sad to say, every widow and widower comes to know a lot about losing a dear one and surviving that loss. Not getting over it but learning to live with it as the pain lessens. As our lives move on.

A Few Points

Later in this book I write about a few points that I want to mention here first:

1. The grief of widowhood is like a chronic condition. Yes, it does get much easier. Yes, joy and peace of mind—and heart—do return. But that grief can flare up both at expected times and at times when it's unexpected.

2. After the death of your spouse you live on the same planet but in a different world.

3. It can be easy to mistakenly assume that if you just had enough faith, if you just prayed harder, if you were just a better Catholic, the grief of widowhood would be swiftly overcome. That isn't true. Yes, our faith, our prayers, and our Catholicism help in many ways. But, no, faith isn't some "get-out-grief-free card."

4. There can be deep comfort in knowing this: either you were going to die first or your spouse was. So either you or your loved one was going to "take the hit" of widowhood. *You're* taking it so—thanks be to God—he or she will never

have to.

Like you were before your spouse's death, your dear one had no idea how huge and awful widowhood would be. And never will know that. Every feeling of loss, fear, and despair so deeply rooted in your widowhood is one he or she will *never* experience.

Your dear spouse is in a state of being that's eternal joy and peace … and is waiting for you to join him or her there. And then you two can, truly, live happily ever after.

About the Book

This isn't a book designed to be read from the first chapter straight through to the last. It might be better to bounce around, from one topic to another, depending on what would be most helpful for you today. For right now.

I didn't write it straight through. A large portion of it is based on newspaper columns and articles I wrote over the first five years after my wife, Monica, died. It reflects how I felt, thought, and prayed over that span. That's why some chapters speak of "a few months ago" and some of three or more years.

Some of the stories I tell and examples I use are based on my own experience. Others come from the widows and widowers in two different spousal-loss support groups I attended.

One More Thing

You and your loved one, you and your family, are in my prayers. God bless you. God give you strength. God give you … peace.

That will come. That will come.

—Bill

1
NO ONE IS PREPARED FOR WIDOWHOOD

I thought I was prepared for widowhood.

I was wrong.

Now, I suspect, no one is ready. That you or I couldn't be.

Widowhood surprises us, and not in a good way. But you already know that if your husband or wife has died. I don't have to tell you. No one does. You know it deep, deep, deep in your heart.

It surprises us if death is unexpected. It surprises us if we knew it was coming.

It's shocking, overwhelming, brain-scrambling, terrifying.

You know that ... now.

And if you're like me, you don't want to know that. You don't want to be a member of a club that no one wants to join. A club called "widowhood."

You may hate that word. And rightly so. From the outside looking in, it means someone who's living life as a widow or widower, as someone whose spouse has died. From the inside looking out, it means so many things, including not being able to imagine your life without him or her.

I couldn't imagine it in those early weeks and months. I sat, I floundered, I prayed, I cried, as slowly, so slowly, hours went by. Days and nights went by. As my life went by without the one who was such a precious and central part of my life.

If you're recently widowed—and that can mean days, weeks, months, or years—you're on a learning curve that seems impossibly steep because, early on, it is nearly impossible. Making it through a morning, an afternoon, an evening, a night. Alone. Yes, others may be around but … you know.

That will change. It won't always be the way it is in the beginning.

Thank God.

But making it through that early period, as you learn to live your life as a widow or widower, takes time. Needs time. Not that time will magically or miraculously "heal all wounds," but over time, and with effort and prayer, that initial rawness lessens.

As you move forward into your new life—new but not chosen or welcomed—you'll learn how to live that life. How to survive and how to figure out what God wants you to do with it.

What God is inviting you to do with it because, now, you know so much more than you did before the love of your life died.

So much you don't want to know.

Dear Lord, I'm overwhelmed. I'm terrified. I'm lost. Dear, Dear Lord, be with me right here, right now.

2
"I'LL TAKE THE HIT"

A few years before Monica got cancer I began praying that she would die before I did. I knew next to nothing about widowhood but I was sure I didn't want her to have to be the survivor.

I would accept that role. Not one I wanted, but if it had to be her or me—and the odds were slim that we'd die together—I wanted to be the partner left behind.

Later, when her diagnosis was terminal, Monica told me she had prayed that she would have time to prepare for death. She wanted to be ready. She did have that time. And she used those ten months oh-so wisely and generously.

So God answered both our prayers just as we had requested but, as is always the case in a happy marriage—no matter how many years a couple has—it wasn't long enough.

In the early months of my widowhood I began consoling myself by saying, "I'll take the hit." One of us had to die before the other, and the one who still lived had to face …

Well, you know what he or she had to face.

You're facing it, even when you can't face it.

I would say to myself, and—I suspect—sometimes out

loud, "I'll take the hit." *I* will be the one to endure the crippling grief I feel right now.

And Monica will never have to.

I'll be the one whose mind won't stop racing, whose heart won't stop breaking, whose soul feels so cold, empty, and alone right now.

And Monica will never have any that.

Despite grieving the death of her father and her grandparents whom she loved so dearly, despite her being a social worker who knew so many things about peoples' personal heartaches and hardships … she didn't have a clue.

You know what I mean.

I began to have the image of us enjoying a lovely, romantic dinner at some swank restaurant. Then the check arrives.

And I pick it up.

When it comes to widowhood, in every marriage, it's the remaining spouse who picks up the check at the end of the meal.

Who takes the hit.

When I hurt so much, I was doing just that and was so very, very glad she *wasn't* doing it right then. Time and again, that thought, that truth, consoled me.

It still does.

I suspect it always will … till we meet again.

The thought of that glorious reunion consoles me, too. We have a lot of catching up to do. And all the time in eternity to do it.

Thank you, Dear Lord, for sparing my dear ____________ from having to endure widowhood. Thank you for letting me be the one to take the hit.

3
ON YOUR PILGRIMAGE CALLED "GRIEF"

It was about six months after Monica died and, in some ways, it seemed like years. In others, only yesterday. And that timeline could shift at any moment, with no apparent regularity or reason.

Being a writer, I wanted my first twelve months of widowhood to have label or a theme. A rookie year. A novitiate. A retreat. A journey, A pilgrimage.

A good friend and "veteran" widow of ten years liked that last one best and so I focused on looking at it in that way. (As in any situation, "veterans" have a lot of wisdom to offer newcomers.)

—A pilgrimage implies movement. I can't stand still although some days I spend a good deal of time resting. Grieving can take a surprising amount of energy even when I feel as if I'm accomplishing so little.

—I'm making my way through unfamiliar—sometimes foreign and frightening—surroundings. Now I write the checks for the monthly bills. Now, in the evening, the house is very quiet.

—There are stops, stations, along the way where I pause

and pray and consider. Remember and grieve. Realize how my life is still so richly blessed and give thanks. There are places that bring tears and places that spark laughter.

—I meet people. Some are new pilgrims like me, others are guides who have been on this path for a long time and remember their first few weeks, months, years. All of us have a similar story to tell but each story is unique.

—I need daily nourishment. Yes, food for physical health but also professional help and the help of family and friends for emotional and spiritual health. I need the grace of God through the sacraments and through his presence in others.

—Day by day, and night by night, I take step after step. Often small steps. Baby steps. Looking back six months I can see I've traveled some distance. Looking around, I can find myself once again in a spot, in a place, I've visited weeks or months ago. It's a winding, circling, confusing path and I don't know where I'm going even as my faith tells me, tries to assure me, that God is with me every step of the way. It says he's leading me and guiding me on this painful journey.

Gently lead me, Lord. Patiently guide me.

4
FAITH I: FAITH DOESN'T ELIMINATE GRIEF

It's can be easy to think if you just had more faith then you wouldn't be grieving so much. Coupled with that, you can blame yourself for having such a hard time because you're sure you just aren't *using* the little faith you do have.

It seems that, one way or another, your misery is *your* fault. Caused by *your* weakness. *Your* sin.

You think of those widowed "stalwarts" in your family or parish and you're sure they didn't have this much trouble after the death of their spouses. Why not? They had and used their faith. *Faith!*

So if you just put more trust in God then ... .

Let's call "time out" here for two simple but horrible truths that you're just discovering.

First, you had no idea what those "stalwarts" were dealing with as they seemed to cruise through life after a few weeks or months. Now you know a lot more about spousal-loss grief. Now you know very, very often most widows and widowers are mum on the subject in public or even among family members. And then they go home and cry. Or they stay home and cry.

Second, faith doesn't eliminate grief. Let's say that again: faith doesn't eliminate grief. Yes, it can truly help you but, no, it's not a magical or mystical free pass. No widow or widower who had a happy marriage gets a free pass.

At the same time, it's not uncommon for a Catholic widow or widower of a few years to recall, "I don't know how I would have gotten through that without my faith."

I feel that way. I found comfort and hope in Catholicism's belief in "the Communion of Saints [*some of us in heaven. others in purgatory (preparing to enter heaven), some of us still here on earth*], … the resurrection of the body [*for everyone at the end of time!*], and life everlasting." To quote the Nicene Creed.

Amen!

But … .

My, oh my, how I hurt during that early period of grief. I hurt like I had never hurt before and I hope (pray) I never hurt that way again. Was it because of my lack of faith? No. Why do I feel bold (confident, cocky) enough to say that?

I didn't stop believing in those teachings, those dogmas, right after Monica died. I clung to them even more. She and I could still be together as members of that "communion."

And someday, at the end of time, her body would be resurrected, just as Jesus' was on Easter Sunday. Mine will rise, too. (I really doubt I'm going to still be ticking at the Second Coming.)

And life everlasting? Count me in!

Then why didn't my faith spare me from the pain of grieving over a loved one's death? Why doesn't it do that for you?

I don't know. I don't think anyone does. It, unfortunately, seems to fall under the heading of "it's a mystery." It's not as if your spousal-loss grief would *not* be a mystery if had more faith or were a better Catholic.

If you had more faith, if you were a better Catholic, would you understand Transubstantiation, that is, bread and wine becoming the body and blood, soul and divinity, of Christ?

No, you would not.

No human, except Jesus, did. Or, I'm willing to bet, ever will. While on earth. (I like to think heaven will include a lot of "ah-ha moments." "Oh! Now I get it.")

Your grief is under the larger category of "Why does an all-loving God allow suffering?" Yes, many saints and scholars have written about that, and what they say can help in our understanding, but … it's a mystery.

We don't know what God knows. Sometimes we don't know, and certainly don't understand, what God does.

But!

God does know you. God does understand you. And, always, always, always, God does love you.

Right here. Right now. In your pain, your confusion, your fear.

Right here.

Right now.

I don't need to know all the answers, Lord, but please ease my pain.

5
FAITH II: GRIEF AND FAITH AT CHRISTMAS

On the first Christmas after Monica died I knew she would be "home for Christmas." Her heavenly home. But I wanted her here. On earth. In the home we created during the thirty-eight years of our marriage. I wanted her sharing that day with our children and grandchildren. Sharing that day with me.

Yes, as I said in the previous chapter, I believe in the Communion of Saints, the resurrection of the body, and life everlasting but still . . . .

Death is awful. (Or put more bluntly: death sucks.)

After her death in early January of that year I had thought a lot about death. I thought about it whether I wanted to or not. (I'm sure the same holds true for you.) And I thought about faith. About phrases and hymns and teachings and beliefs that used to be so easy. So almost-automatically comforting.

Yes, Monica's "with me" all the time now. Yes, since she's with God, she's with Christ in a particular way in the Eucharist at Mass. Yes, she's free from pain and worry and fear. But still . . . .

Death is awful.

Grief is awful.

And faith doesn't eliminate either one.

I think those of us who are grieving—especially on a special day like Christmas or a birthday or anniversary—can be tempted to think "If I only had more faith, if I only better used the faith I have, I wouldn't feel so horrible. This wouldn't be so horrible."

But I don't think that's true. And, as is so often the case, it's Mary—our Blessed Mother—who shows us that just isn't so. Certainly no one (except her Son) had more faith than she did. No one better used that faith. Better lived that faith. But even her heart was "pierced by a sword" (see Lk 2:35).

Rightfully so, she's known under the title of "Our Lady of Sorrows."

It's one she earned. One she lived.

Scripture doesn't tell us, but who could doubt she deeply grieved the death of her beloved Joseph? Of her darling little boy, Jesus?

It seems safe to speculate that at times she pondered in her heart that this wasn't how her life was "*supposed* to be." How she had thought and prayed it *would* be.

As you're grieving the loss of a loved one this Christmas, you may find yourself thinking this isn't how your life was "*supposed* to be." How you thought and prayed it *would* be.

But it is.

And there's no changing that.

If you're grieving the loss of a loved one this Christmas, I say to you what I said to myself during those early years of widowhood: Be gentle with yourself. Be patient with yourself. Be kind to yourself.

Do what you want to do and can do when it comes to this holiday and holy day. Accept the fact that perhaps, this year, you can't do what you want to do or think you "should" do. Not now. Not yet.

And that's OK.

It well may be that since the death of your loved one, you've grown in wisdom, age, grace … and faith.

But still … .

Widow Mary, Our Lady of Sorrows, pray for me, pray with me.

6

GRIEF: THE MULTI-HEADED MONSTER

It was a little more than a month after Monica died that I jotted this down:

Widowhood is "like making your way through a dense forest, without trails. Others can offer help and can talk about how they made it through, but your forest is *your* forest: all those unique parts of your relationship with your loved one."

The forest I pictured was like those in western Washington state with all kinds of evergreens packed closely together and all types of underbrush closing in on every side.

A few months later, in a support group, one widow said she thought it was like getting dropped into the ocean. For a long time she was underwater, fighting to get to the surface. And then, after weeks if not months, she reached it and could take a deep breath. But … looking around she couldn't see any land. She didn't know exactly where she was or which way to go.

Even though *you* know what happened, what you're going through is hard to describe. It's an overwhelming jumble that … .

Sometimes words or an image help a bit but, at other times—because it's such a unique experience—there's no perfect image to say what it feels like for you. There are no words that do it justice.

It's not that you aren't imaginative enough. It's not that you aren't verbal enough.

My forest description kind of worked for me. Right then. The widow's ocean analogy probably worked for her. That day.

But widowhood can be a shapeshifter. This in the morning, that in the afternoon.

In the morning it makes you feel exhausted and so you stay in bed.

In the afternoon it forces you to deal with at least some of the mounds of death-related paperwork sitting on your dining room table.

If you asked a dozen recent widows and widowers "What's it like when your spouse dies?" you'd probably get a dozen different answers. And if you asked them a month later, probably quite a few would have a different description.

Widowhood can be a multi-headed monster. You don't know which head you're going to have to deal with, or avoid, right now. And you don't know when and where a brand new one is going to pop up and go after you.

In my own experience, and in the experiences of many widows and widowers: It's not always going to be like that.

Over time, the heads become familiar and some all but disappear. Over time, a new one can be more easily handled because you've learned how to deal with new ones. You know what's worked in the past and what hasn't.

I'm reminded of a woman in one of my groups whose husband had been dead for close to a year. She told us that, out of the blue, a feeling of deep grief came storming back after she had had some days when things felt better. Not perfect, but better.

She told us that she said out loud, "Oh, it's you." As if grief were a person. An unwanted and unwelcomed visitor. But not one unknown to her.

She knew, at some point, it would leave.

And it did. Not permanently. But for now. And feeling no grief right now is very, very good.

You're learning this. You've already learned some of it and you'll learn more.

The Latin expression is *experientia docet*: experience teaches.

Widowhood, such a horrible experience or complex web of experiences, is a powerful teacher. With so many very tough lessons.

Down the road you'll know a lot about widowhood. You'll have made it through so many lessons, tests, pop quizzes, and homework. You'll know how to survive, to move forward, and to find a new peace.

Dearest Lord, please give me a moment of peace today.

7

"I HAVE AN IDEA OF WHAT YOU'RE GOING THROUGH"

About half a year after Monica died I sent an email to the widow of a high school classmate who had passed away four years earlier. I introduced myself, told her some stories about him from "the old days," and promised to pray for her and their children.

When she wrote back, so very grateful for my note, she began with: "I have an idea of what you're going through."

And I knew *she* knew. Not my exact circumstances, challenges, or private grief, but what it's like to lose a spouse.

Only *you* know exactly what you're going through. Fellow widows and widowers have an idea, but each one's story is unique. They know widowhood from the inside looking out but not from what was the "inside" of your relationship with your spouse or all the other particular circumstances of your loss and your grieving.

Widening that circle a bit, there are others who have a notion of what you experienced and what you're experiencing. They may have lost a parent, a child, a sibling, or other close relative. They may have lost a dear friend.

But, again, unless you've lost a child, you can't have the depth of understanding of someone who has. Or a sibling. And so on.

I was in a group facilitated by a terrific social worker whose father had died suddenly when she was in her late teens. Later, she worked with hospice and loss for many years, leading spousal-loss groups and providing individual counseling.

She was very, very good at what she did but more than once she told us, "You're the experts here."

And we were. She helped us move along those early paths of widowhood because she knew them well but she had never walked them herself. And she knew that made a difference. A big difference.

She taught us as she continued to learn from us.

On the other hand, you may have encountered some people who assume they know exactly what you're going through. That your grief is identical to (or not as bad as) the grief they've experienced.

More than one group member mentioned how maddening it was when someone equated the loss of a husband or wife to that person's loss of his or her cat.

(That *always* brought a strong response from groups members, even among those who loved their dog or cat.)

Over the last few years I've realized that it's true the person who lost a pet is "filled" with grief, just as a widow or widower is. But I strongly suspect (and would bet my bottom dollar on), widowhood involves a deeper grief.

On the surface they could look identical. Filled to the brim. But spousal loss is incredibly deep and wide. In those early days, weeks, months, and sometimes years, it seems it has no bottom. No edge. Or perhaps it does and that's where you seem to be living your life. On the bottom. On the edge.

Grief can't be measured. It can't be quantified. And it can fluctuate within you from day to day. From hour to hour. But … .

Its intensity does decrease. Peace does surface. Joy does return. Not identical to what had been, but a new peace. A new joy. A new life. Your new life.

Out of the depths of grief I cry to you, Lord;
Lord, hear my prayer!

8
THE COST OF YOUR HAPPY MARRIAGE

It doesn't help that family and friends who still have their spouses may be clueless. And, sometimes, seemingly thoughtless.

Then again, those could be indicators that what you had, and miss so terribly much, isn't what he or she has. Maybe that person doesn't have a happy marriage. Maybe it's a very unhappy one.

My own experiences of being with recent widows and widowers is skewed. Generally, those who gathered around a table at a spousal-loss support group meeting were ones who *did* have a happy marriage. (Not a perfect one. No couple has a perfect marriage.)

But I know that some survivors see widowhood as a welcome escape from a tremendously unhappy or even abusive relationship. One social worker told our group of going to visit a new widow and expressing concern about how she was doing. The woman nodded cordially to all the questions she was being asked and then gently said, "Oh, honey, you don't have to worry about me. He was a real S.O.B."

It wouldn't surprise me if you've run into some folks

who, in trying to look on the sunny side of your new life, say things that cut deeply.

"You're so lucky. Now you can play tennis anytime you want."

That's what one new widow was told.

"Lucky"?

"Tennis"!

Or … .

"You get to go home to a nice, quiet house and relax. I have to go fix his dinner."

The woman who shared that story angrily shook her head and said she would give *anything* to be able to go home and fix dinner for her husband.

Another talked about how hard it was to see a couple arguing in public.

A second widow agreed. "I just want to tell them to stop that and appreciate what they still have," she said.

"I *did* do that!" the first widow said.

I myself have become more aware of older married couples attending Mass together, walking through the neighborhood, or shopping at the local grocery store. Sometimes at Mass they hold hands during the Our Father. Sometimes on a walk they're enjoying a quiet conversation. And sometimes in the store they're studying a shopping list.

I envy them but once in a while the thought occurs to me that they don't know what lies ahead. For one of them. Then I say a silent, little prayer for whichever one that will be.

You and I have an idea of what he or she will face. Alone. Yes—please, God—that will be with the help and the prayers of many others but … alone.

If you're a recent widow or widower, I'll tell you something you may not know. Or may not, at this point on your personal pilgrimage, believe. In my own experience, after four years of widowhood, it's gotten better. The grief is much less frequent and much less intense. (I've thanked

God it doesn't stay at that off the scale level of early widowhood.)

For me, there's been a gradual change. A lessening. No waking up "cured" or having it "all behind me."

But easier to function. To breathe. To think. To pray. To continue to move into my new life … as a widower.

To remember, with joy, moments from my marriage.

To thank God that I had such a happy, happy marriage for thirty-eight years.

And to point out to him, one more time, there weren't enough.

Holy Spirit, Great Comforter and Consoler,
help me sleep better.

9
DEALING WITH GRIEF ISN'T ONE-SIZE-FITS-ALL

The woman in my support group was describing how much her husband's chair meant to her. It was where he always sat in the living room when they watched television in the evening. He sat in his, she sat in hers.

Now his was empty. Always empty.

But, she said, she would look at it, remember him sitting there, and talk to him now about her day. Not that she was having visions or was delusional, not that she was holding some kind of séance, but it was a way for her to feel close to him.

It gave her a sense of peace.

Others at the meeting nodded in agreement and then one fellow spoke up. A big guy who didn't talk very often.

"My wife and I had recliners," he said. "I just couldn't look at hers. So finally I just picked it up and carried out to my truck. I loaded it in the back, drove to the dump, and threw it out there."

There might have been a few gasps. It was obvious some at the table couldn't imagine doing such a thing. And, it seemed, they thought no one should do such a thing.

But it worked for him. It helped him.

And it was a good, a startling, reminder that what works for one widow or widower may be a horrible idea for another.

One found comfort in having a spouse's chair in the living room. The other found peace by getting it out of there.

As the months went by and I was still going to two different support groups, I began to realize more and more how one size doesn't fit all when it comes to widowhood. When it comes to mine. When it comes to yours.

At another session, a widow and widower who had been attending meetings for several months had advice for two new members. Here, specifically, they said, is what the neophytes, the newbies, *had* to do.

Well … no.

A thought occurred to me.

"One thing that helps me," I said, "is to remember that what works for one person may be a poor choice for another. It's like being newly married. The two of you have to figure out what works for you. And what doesn't work. Some couples like to go out often. Some prefer to stay home most of the time. Some enjoy an activity and think every couple will. Like … ."

I was holding an internal debate. Which to use for an example? Bowling or square dancing?

"Like if you and your spouse love square dancing. And you tell a newly-married couple that if they don't start square dancing and stick with it, well, then they're not going to have a strong and happy marriage. That's because it's helped you have a strong and happy marriage."

I saw some folks nodding and then one fellow gave a little smile and said, "My wife and I loved square dancing."

There was a lot of laughter. (Amazingly, there was often a lot of laughter at a spousal-loss support group meeting. And, not surprisingly, a lot of tears, too.)

"Well, shoot," I said. "I was debating. Bowling. Square dancing. Bowling. Square dancing. I should have picked bowling."

Dear Holy Spirit, give me the wisdom to find my path on this pilgrimage and to make my way forward.

10

YOUR INSIDE VIEW OF "THE STAGES OF GRIEF"

Even before your spouse died you probably had heard of the stages of grief and maybe could even list a few of them. Then, too, you may have gone through them yourself after the death of a loved one.

The five traditional ones—from Swiss psychiatrist Elisabeth Kübler-Ross in her 1969 book *On Death and Dying*—are denial, anger, bargaining, depression, and acceptance.

Kübler-Ross was a pioneer in the field of working with the terminally ill and her categories for the dying, and their grieving survivors, are helpful but easily misunderstood. There's a popular misconception that the griever goes through those stages like a kid goes through school. Done with one grade, on to next. Never to return to an earlier one.

She later clarified she made a mistake listing them as if there were a 1-2-3 progression. They could come in any order. Some not at all. Some repeated time and again.

In other words, she said what you now know to be true: grief is messy.

As one social worker leading our grief group explained to us, others in the field of grief have used different metaphors to describe your pilgrimage. Grief comes "in waves." Grief is a "line that coils back over itself" again and again as it moves forward.

You know what it's like: it's like something you've never experienced before. Not to this depth. Not to this breadth. Not to this length.

The truth is you may or not be done with denial, for example, when you seem no longer to be denying your spouse's death. That stage, that wave, that point on a bedspring-like path may return.

It helped me to hear about that during the first half year after Monica died. It let me off the hook if I had somehow returned to one of the stages from which I thought I had "graduated." So I hadn't somehow failed. It was how this complicated mess called grief … progressed?

Yes. Progressed. In baby steps. Not infrequently with that old feeling of one small step forward, many (large) steps back. There I was, returned to where I had been when? A week ago? A month ago? Half a year ago?

But at some point I realized (thanks be to God) I wasn't back to *exactly* where I had been. Whatever stage or feeling I was now encountering wasn't unfamiliar to me. I had come across it—it had crushed me—before and I had ... what?

What had helped me then? What might help me now?

This new meeting might look the same, it might feel the same, but I wasn't the same. I now had some experience dealing with, living with for a time, whatever ugly, fearsome bit of grief had once again plowed into me.

I had slayed that dragon. And this new encounter surprised me, and upset me, but this wasn't *that* dragon. This was—what?—his little brother? He wasn't as tough and he had less endurance. Now I was tougher and had more.

A confession here. The dragon metaphor didn't occur to me until I just wrote these words. I think it's a good one so

I include it here. What I really thought, at the time, was when I felt as if I were back to where I had been I was at …

A different McDonald's.

I was on my pilgrimage, on my path, and this "stage" that had popped up wasn't the same one I had dealt with earlier. At first glance, all McDonald's restaurants look the same but they aren't. There are differences.

And, if I thought about it, I could remember what helped me the last time I had had to deal with one. Hmm. Last time I ordered a chocolate shake. (Last time I slowed down and gave myself more breaks. Took naps. Dropped any unnecessary commitments. For a time.)

I could try that this time. If it worked, great! If it didn't, I could try something else. Something that just might work this time. And if not, maybe the next time.

(My apologies to all McDonald's restaurants. I'm not saying you're really like denial, anger, or any of the other traditional five. I enjoy the food!)

Your grief is *your* grief. Your pilgrimage is *your* pilgrimage. Books, groups, websites, fellow widows and widowers, can help you but no one can do it *for* you.

Even God doesn't do it *for* you.

But he's always with you. Through *all* your stages, waves, or loops.

Right here. Right now.

Thank you, Lord, that I'm learning more about living with my loss
and my grief so I can better live with my loss
and my grief. I just wish these lessons weren't so hard.
Sometimes, so brutal.

11
THE GIFT OF TEARS

I seldom cried as an adult. And I shed no tears immediately after Monica died. Not during her funeral. Not at her burial.

My lack of tears didn't bother me. Somehow I knew they would come. And they did, but only when I was alone or it was unlikely they'd be noticed by others. (Wiping—or blotting—my eyes at Mass, for example.)

I don't know why my tears came that way. Why they still do but, now, not as frequently. I wasn't trying to hide them from others. And I certainly told others that I had been crying. Frequently. Deeply.

I suspect that crying, as a part of grief, can be very individualistic, just as all facets of grief can be. There's no "right" or "wrong" way to shed tears. When and how you cry isn't something to be determined or controlled by someone else. Or by what you think others may be thinking about you.

I will say this: crying was a wonderful release for me during those early times of widowhood. As an (almost) non-crier for most of my adult life, I had no idea how helpful it could be. Which is a little funny, in a way, because Monica was always big on crying. (That sounds nicer than saying "she was a big crier.")

As a rookie crier, and a rookie griever, I discovered my "Monica Moments" could be divided into three stages. As I write this, I realize for the first time, that when I cried I was following Monica's example. But when I came up with the term I meant I was thinking about her and feeling so terrible. (You know how that goes.)

Stage 1: tears well up in my eyes and need to be wiped or blotted.

Stage 2: tears roll down my cheeks and are wiped away.

Stage 3: tears rolls down my cheeks and I get a very runny nose. The tears have to be wiped away and the nose has to be blown … vigorously.

Obviously, I had become very, very familiar with the nuances of my weeping.

But there's more.

When my siblings and I were teenagers and heading out the door, Mom would always ask, "Do you have a hankie and a dime to call home?" (That dates me.) Since then I've made sure to carry a handkerchief in my pants pocket. (And now my cell phone, too.)

Soon after Monica's death I started carrying two hankies. A big Monica Moment Stage 3 could completely use up one of them.

I've told others about these categories and sometimes a person will ask, "What's a Stage 4?"

I don't know. I suspect it would be gasping for breath and/or being unable to stand. But those never happened to me. I know other people have experienced both.

Again, that doesn't mean one of us is crying wrong. Isn't being sad enough or is being too sad.

I cry when I cry. Just as I take a drink of water when I'm thirsty. No one can measure my grief and tell me now it's time to cry or now it's not time to cry. And no one can tell me now I'm thirsty or now I'm not thirsty.

Of course the same holds true for you.

Crying, the ability to cry, is a gift from God.
It's meant to be used when and how you need it.

Thank you, Dear Lord, for the "gift" of tears.
(And for vigorous nose-blowing, too.)

12
MORE THAN "ACQUAINTED" WITH GRIEF

A snippet from Scripture popped into my head: "he was a man of sorrows, and acquainted with grief."

At least I thought it was from the Bible so I looked it up. Isaiah 53:3. Some translations don't used that phrasing but I really like its King James Version best. That's not to say I "like" it. It more that I'm quite familiar with it. From the inside looking out.

"Sorrow" and I were roommates. "Grief" and I were on a first-name basis.

I was a man *filled with sorrow* and *more than* acquainted with grief. To use a modern idiom, it was my default setting. I'm not saying I wallowed in sorrow and grief. That seems to imply in some way it was my fault or I enjoyed it or wanted to use it to my advantage.

(Grief, an "advantage." Ha!)

It was more like I was a victim of a tsunami of both of them. A giant wave that knocked me head over heels and left me completely disoriented. That swept me up and then dragged me out into the unknown.

Deeper into widowhood. Farther from Monica.

I'm no Scripture scholar. Not even a very good student of it. I had to look up that verse from Isaiah to find out what the prophet was talking about. As you probably know, it was Jesus and his passion and death.

In a way, the loss of your dear spouse and what comes next happen is the opposite order of that. After the *death* of your husband or wife, you enter *your* passion. Your personal "Way of the Cross," with the cross being widowhood. Yes, some widows and widowers live—survive—only a few hours, days, weeks, or months. Some make it for a year or two. Most of us get through those initial years and, if we're young enough, may be around for decades.

Here's some good news. Through those early years and beyond, your "way" grows less painful.

Step by step. Day by day. Night by night. As, gradually, it becomes week by week. Month by month. Year by year.

The sorrow and grief slowly diminish. On their own time. In their own way.

And, step by step, they're replaced with joy and purpose.

Often the transition, the transformation, is so subtle it's almost unnoticed except by looking back and recalling those first days, weeks, months, and years. Then you realize where you are now on your "way," on your "pilgrimage," is quite a distance from where you first began it.

Sorrow is no longer your roommate. Grief drops by far less often and doesn't stay as long.

Today, Dear Lord, I pray for those who are just beginning their widowhood.

13
THE MANY ROLES YOUR SPOUSE PLAYED

One reason the death of your spouse is devastating is that he or she filled so many roles in your everyday life.

I kept bumping into that, crashing into that, in the early months after Monica's death. It surprised me, not that she did so much, but how over thirty-eight years of marriage we had shared our "couple times" together and divided so many household duties.

I started to make a list of them and I would include it here but ... . A lot of what I did during that time is lost, or was set aside in some "safe place" so I'd be sure to easily find it later.

Ah, well.

No doubt you and your sweetie had your own shared "couple times" and your own division of duties. One of our "couple times" was in the evening. We'd watch television, mute it during the commercials, and visit with each other. Soon after she died I couldn't watch "our" favorite shows. (And I couldn't focus long enough to follow a one-hour plot. Added to that, God forbid any had a storyline that included death, cancer, or marriage.)

Not that we didn't talk to each other during a program itself. She might begin to ask, "Is that the guy who … ?" And I would interrupt and say, "No." I knew who she meant. She knew I knew whom she meant. On the other hand, if one of us came up with another movie or TV show an actor had been in, that was met with a "Well done" or "Nice."

It was a game we played. One we were both good, or bad, at. One we both enjoyed. Even now, when I get one "right"—especially an obscure one—I might look at her picture that's near the TV and say, "Pretty good, huh?"

I have no doubt every married couple has its own "couple time" and its own division of duties.

One or the other: pays the bills each month, does the annual taxes, cooks, does the laundry, takes care of solicitors at the front door, grills hamburgers on the patio, gets all the holiday decorations out of the attic or garage or basement (and returns them there), fixes a leaky faucet, sews a button back on a shirt, and on and on.

And on.

Many widows have told me, "I had no idea how much he did. And he was so fast at it. He made it look so easy." One came to a meeting and was happy to report a victory. "I fixed the dryer," she said. "How did you learn that?" we asked. She sat up straighter and smiled. "A YouTube video!"

Not a few new widowers have said, "I'm living on toast and scrambled eggs now. I eat out a lot."

Not that the division of labor was based rigidly on traditional male/female roles. But there was a division. One that, over the years of their marriage, worked well for them. (Or that each learned to live with.)

There was a different kind of role, too. Lover, friend, traveling companion, Number 1 Fan, sounding board, defender, hand-holder, memory keeper and sharer … . And more. A long list. A personal list. In some ways, a private list. A cherished list but, now, one that can hurt.

I feel safe to say that if what a couple had was a loving, happy marriage then it takes that widow or widower time—and tears—to begin to adjust to a spouse no longer filling all those roles.

Just as you loved your spouse for so many reasons, you miss him or her for so many, too.

God gave you that multitalented, multifaceted, "multi-wonderful" husband or wife. Not one in a million, your spouse was one in all of creation.

Thank you, Lord, for my dear, dear ________________. I can't count all the ways I love him/her.

14

ANSWERING JESUS' CALL TO DO LESS

I've noticed it's no longer necessary for me to focus on Jesus saying, "Whoever wishes to come after me must deny himself, take up his cross, and follow me" (Mt 16:24).

I don't need a reminder that there's a new cross, an inescapable cross, in my life. It's been there since Monica died.

I've come to realize what I need to pay attention to, what I need to remind myself of, is Christ telling the apostles to "come away … and rest a while" (Mk 6:31).

I can't set down the "cross" of widowhood. But I can cut myself some slack.

I not only *can* do less. Sometimes I *should* do less.

"I'll never forget what you told me," a widow—a fellow "club member"—said to me when each of us was closing in on the one-year anniversary of our spouse's death.

I confess I was a little worried what my "words of wisdom" might have been.

"You said," she continued, "after your wife had been dead only a short while sometimes you just sat in the living room and did nothing."

She had me. I didn't remember telling her that but I

clearly recalled doing it. Not "shutting down" the engine but … putting it in "park" for a while.

It had been early in my widowhood, during that period when there are so many, many things that have to be done. Bills needed to be paid. Not overdue, but due. Thank-you cards had to be sent to those who had made a donation in Monica's memory to the Friends of St. John the Caregiver. (The non-profit we began in 2005 to help family caregivers.) Then, too, I "should" get to the grocery store, I "should" go take a walk, and on and on.

But I was so tired. Physically, mentally, emotionally, and spiritually.

So I sat. Just sat. Probably not for a long time. Fifteen minutes? Half an hour?

Obviously, it helped since later I had recommended it to a widow.

Still, admitting to "just sitting" can be hard to do because it's far from socially acceptable. A *good* person is a *productive* person. A good person may "just be sitting" but she's praying or he's reading or … . But doing *nothing*?

Yes.

It's OK for you to do that kind of "nothing," especially early into your widowhood. From the outside looking in, it looks suspiciously like a waste of time. Of just … wallowing. From the inside looking out, you're sitting there not just in your living room but in your widowhood. In your grief.

And one of the things every grieving spouse needs to become acclimated to *is* time. And sometimes what a recent—or not-so-recent—widow or widower needs is that "down time." Sometimes our body, our mind, our heart, and our soul (perhaps a combination of all four) knock us down and sit us in that chair.

For a while.

If you've lost your spouse, sometimes doing that kind of "nothing" is doing a *lot*. It's doing what you need to do but, maybe, haven't been allowing yourself to do.

At one group meeting a woman "confessed" she had spent the previous morning in bed. "All morning. Doing nothing."

"Not so," the social worker said softly. "You probably were doing exactly what you *needed* to do."

It's sound advice. Even biblical! Just as he told the apostles, it can be Jesus telling you to "come away … and rest awhile."

In fact, it's doing what, Scripture tells us, Jesus himself did.

He [Jesus] had to pass through Samaria. So he came to a town of Samaria called Sychar, near the plot of land that Jacob had given to his son Joseph. Jacob's well was there. Jesus, tired from his journey, sat down there at the well. It was about noon (John 4:4-6).

He was tired. He sat down.

You're on a journey. Sometimes, a lot of the time, you're tired.

Sit down.

Help me pay attention, Lord, when you tell me to sit down,
to just stop. Help me rest.

15
GOD'S (STUPID) WILL

My mom died a little less than five months after Monica did. It came as no surprise. She had been in a nursing home for more than a year and was ninety-four.

During that time between the two deaths I would go and visit her. We'd have lunch together and then make a stop in the home's chapel. We'd sit side-by-side and hold hands in front of the statue of the Immaculate Conception.

In a strange and new way, Mom and I had become peers. She had a very good idea of what I was going through and I had a better idea of what it had been like for her after Dad had died fifteen years earlier.

One time she gently shook her head and whispered, "God's will."

I leaned in and said, "God's stupid will."

She smiled, knowing my sense of humor came from Dad and knowing I wasn't being blasphemous.

"Well," she whispered, "I wouldn't use that word."

As if she didn't disagree with my assessment, just that she herself wouldn't say it.

Sometimes it can really seem that way.

The death of your spouse makes no sense. It's unfair. It's

… it's … it's beyond words but it's bad, bad, bad, and how could that be God's will? An "all-loving" God!

You may have had a well-meaning family member or friend remind you the death of your spouse was "God's will" or "God's plan." No doubt it was said to bring comfort. No doubt, in some deep ways, it fell short of the mark.

And, because it did, you may have felt a pang of guilt. If the thought of "God's will" or "God's plan" triggered that reaction in you, doesn't that mean you're a bad Catholic?

No. It means you're a human being. Who very well could be a very good Catholic.

Coming to accept God's will isn't the same as always liking God's will. Need some proof of that? Consider Jesus in the Garden of Gethsemane. Knowing very soon he would be arrested, tortured, and executed.

Then Jesus came with them to a place called Gethsemane, and he said to his disciples, "Sit here while I go over there and pray." He took along Peter and the two sons of Zebedee, and began to feel sorrow and distress.

Then he said to them, "My soul is sorrowful even to death. Remain here and keep watch with me."

He advanced a little and fell prostrate in prayer, saying, "My Father, if it is possible, let this cup pass from me; yet, not as I will, but as you will."

When he returned to his disciples he found them asleep. He said to Peter, "So you could not keep watch with me for one hour? Watch and pray that you may not undergo the test. The spirit is willing, but the flesh is weak."

Withdrawing a second time, he prayed again, "My Father, if it is not possible that this cup pass without my drinking it, your will be done!"

Then he returned once more and found them asleep, for they could not keep their eyes open. He left them and withdrew again and prayed a third time, saying the same thing again.

Then he returned to his disciples and said to them, "Are you still sleeping and taking your rest? Behold, the hour is at hand when the Son of Man is to be handed over to sinners. Get up, let us go. Look, my betrayer is at hand" (Mt 26:36-46).

The evangelist Luke described it this way:

He prayed, saying, "Father, if you are willing, take this cup away from me; still, not my will but yours be done." And to strengthen him an angel from heaven appeared to him. [He was in such agony and he prayed so fervently that his sweat became like drops of blood falling on the ground.] (Lk 22: 41-44).

Matthew has Jesus saying three times that he didn't like the plan. Luke says even an angel couldn't ease Jesus' deep pain. No wonder the scene is called the "Agony in the Garden."

And now you find yourself in the "Agony of Widowhood." Like Jesus, you say you don't want it. Repeatedly. Unlike Jesus, you can't understand this "will," this "plan," the same way he did.

Dear Jesus, help me accept and do my Heavenly Father's will even when I hate what he's asking of me.

16
EVEN JESUS HAD HELP CARRYING HIS CROSS

Yes, "If anyone wishes to come after me, he must deny himself and take up his cross daily and follow me" (Lk 9:23).

Yes, "I have the strength for everything through him [God] who empowers me" (Phil 4:13).

But maybe no—quite possibly no—"God doesn't give you more than you can handle." It's a popular quote ... but not scriptural. It's religiously cultural and, most times, meant to be helpful. Comforting. Encouraging. Empowering.

Meant to be.

On the other hand, perhaps like Jesus on his way to Calvary, you need some help. Perhaps sometimes you need your own "Simon of Cyrene." And perhaps sometimes the strength God is giving you is the wisdom and courage to ask for help from others. To accept the help others offer.

So, yes, it can be said God never gives you more than you can handle because he gives the rest of us the opportunity, the privilege, and the obligation to help you. In particular, many of us who are further into our widowhood *want* to help you. To listen. To speak of our own journey. To hold your hand. To hold you in our hearts and pray for you at a time when your heart is so broken.

Ours continue to heal, but will always be scarred.

This isn't to say it's *always* best to look for help as quickly as possible and *always* accept all offers of help when it comes to your grief. It was several months before I went to a five-part "class" on it. A couple more after that before I reached out or responded to peers who were widowed.

My early widowhood was … a mess. A mishmash. A just getting through the day. Through the many parts of every day. You know. The thought of adding anything to that was overwhelming. Impossible. The informal support I received then was from family. A visit. A phone call. An email. (No texts. That was a skill I learned later. Monica was the one with the cell phone. I had never used one.)

Knowing I was in loved ones' thoughts and prayers was a powerful comfort. They hadn't forgotten, forsaken, me a week after Monica died. A month. A year. Or more. They still remember what Monica and I had. And what I lost.

The death of a spouse is two losses: one loses his or her life; the other, the life they had.

One enters eternal life.

The other, with the grace of God coupled with the assistance of others, begins fashioning a new life on earth. A different life.

Bit by bit. Step by step. Grace by grace.

When I'm ready and able, Lord,
help me accept more help from others.

17
TELLING YOUR STORY

There was a time, not long after Monica's death, that it felt as if all I was doing was sitting down at my laptop and typing: Monica died. Monica died. Monica died.

In a way, I was. I had called her mother the morning after Monica's death and sent emails to family and friends that day. Soon after that I was working on her obituary.

At some point in that early-days-of-loss fog, I wrote pieces for: the St. John the Caregiver website. (the non-profit we began in 2005.); *My Daily Visitor.* (the daily devotional magazine we had edited for ten years): and Catholic News Service (where we had written a monthly family column for twenty years).

Each of those three had a particular audience, each—in one way or another—had known Monica and known she had been terminally ill, and so each needed an announcement and personal message from me tailored to it.

Maybe you've experienced, or are experiencing the same thing in your own way. Not so much putting the news in writing but telling the story, your story, to family and friends who have called. Who were at the funeral or memorial service. People from work or the parish or the neighborhood.

One way or another, there are times when those encounters can include telling your story.

And, looking back, maybe you can recognize times when someone who was deeply grieving had told you his or her story.

I can think of two. In both instances I was at the husband's memorial service and signed the guest book but didn't get the opportunity to say a few words to the widow. Who am I kidding? Most likely I didn't take the opportunity or make the effort to say a few words. Most likely I didn't know what to say so I avoided having to say anything.

(My, how that's changed. My, how I've changed. Just one of the pieces of knowledge that come from the hard, hard lessons of losing a spouse.)

In each of those cases, it was the widow, my friend, who called me a month or so later. She had seen my name in the guest book and was sorry we hadn't had a chance to visit. (Now, I know, one of us was … hiding. Now, I'm amazed that she could remember that we hadn't talked.)

I was touched, and honored, that she would reach out to me. And when she did, what she did, was tell me the story of her husband's death. What happened on that day. No, not everything but, I was sure, more than just a general summary.

There were details, some of which I remember to this day. Some of which, I know now, she needed to share with others. A select few others. With others she trusted, and with whom she wanted to share the story. And, I know now, needed to share with others.

For me, writing about and telling others about Monica's death was a way that news, that sad, sad reality, that devastating truth, gradually sank in for me. Sank into me.

Into my mind, my heart, my soul.

It was what, for a time, I thought was going to sink me.

Obviously, I'm still telling it. Still, in some ways, need to tell it. (Thank you for listening!)

And, obviously, it didn't "sink" me. Maimed me, yes. Sank me completely, no.

You may find it helps you to tell your story. Over and over. To people you trust. To people who care for you and about you. Folks who will listen to the telling … and the retelling.

And you may feel you're sinking. You probably are, into the depths of grief. A cold, dark, foreign, frightening, and lonely place.

Sinking but not permanently sunk. Not condemned forever, not damned, to that place. To that way of being. Your life will become warmer, lighter, more familiar, and far less frightening and lonely.

Your life has changed and will continue to change. I suppose I could use some annoying cliché here and say "you have no way to go but up" but widowhood isn't a cliché. Grief isn't a cliché. And, like your story, how you find your way, how you make your way, forward—or "up"—is a story that's yours alone.

It's one that you will come to tell, if you choose to, just as I—five years after Monica's death—am telling mine here and now.

Dear Lord, the story of my life includes such a devastating loss.
Be with me now.

18
THE NEED TO TALK … AND LISTEN

The day after Monica found out her cancer had returned and she had at most a year to live, she signed up for hospice. That's the kind of person she was.

Among the services available to her were a visiting nurse and visiting social worker. Over the next ten months we got to know, and deeply respect, both of them. I'll always be grateful for what they did and how they did it to help Monica, our children, and me.

Most times I would be in the living room with Monica when either healthcare professional stopped by, but once my dear wife arranged for me to meet with the social worker by myself. Monica, a social worker herself, said it would be good for that professional and me to talk without her being present.

I said OK but I wasn't convinced. I had no secrets. I had no concerns I couldn't bring up with her in the room.

If you were a caregiver for your spouse, you know how blurry parts of that time can be. But I do remember this: The social worker advised me that after Monica died I would need someone to talk to. It could be in a formal setting (a social worker, counselor, or facilitated support group); or it could be in an informal setting (a family member or friend).

After widowhood hit me in the head, I realized she was right. I needed to talk and I needed someone to listen. (I'm pretty sure a lot, if not most, of us widowed folks do some talking out loud when we're alone.)

I hadn't realized how much I relied on Monica to fill that role until—just when I needed her most—she was gone.

You may have discovered the same has been true for you and your spouse.

As I wrote in the previous chapter, part of it for me—and for many of us—is to simply, or not so simply, tell and retell the story of my loved one's death. Part of it for me was simply, or not so simply, to tell my story to someone who would listen and not jump in with "answers."

Over time the need to talk continued but the topic expanded. The topics. It was what was happening now after a month, two months, six months had passed. It was what was going on with me but also with my children and grandchildren. It was about new challenges that sprang up from my recent widowhood.

It was feeling as if I had made the tiniest bit of headway and then—*wham!*—finding myself feeling as I had in the very early days.

Looking back, I suppose I was like someone who had been dropped into a foreign land. Stumbling around in my new, unchosen, and unwanted life took so much effort. And I so dearly missed my former life. A life to which I could never return.

What a relief it was, what a joy it was, to find fellow immigrants. Some who had learned to move forward and function in this new land. Some who, like me, were still stumbling as they adjusted.

Longtime or recently widowed, they walked with me, baby step by baby step, listening to me and sharing with me parts of their own story, their own path, their own pilgrimage.

Dear Lord, help me find people I can talk to about all this, and help me hear what they're saying.

19

FINDING FORMAL AND INFORMAL SUPPORT

At a time in your life when you're so terribly lonely it can help to know you don't have to go it alone during that early widowhood period.

Or the later ones either.

Looking back on my own experiences I can see I was so fortunate, so richly blessed, to find both formal and informal support.

The formal was a grief support group associated with the hospice service that helped Monica and the family during the last ten months of her life. I didn't have to search for one, and began taking a once-a-week class for five weeks to learn more about grief. Especially the grief after losing a spouse. More about what to expect. And more about identifying what I was experiencing.

But, at that time, after the classes ended, there was no follow-up group available. By then it had been about five months since Monica had died and I knew I needed some kind of support group.

In time, like Goldilocks, I found one that was just right. After sampling a couple that were just … wrong. For me.

(See Appendix 2 for "Tips on Finding a Support Group.")

Not long after that the social worker from the class began a support group for her "graduates." That was how I ended up in two groups. About eighteen months later the "class" group formally disbanded but many of its members continue to meet several times a year for a potluck lunch. (I bring the (store-bought) cheesecake.)

None of this is to say a group is for everyone. I found it very helpful, even though there were many days when I didn't want to go. By then I knew how much I benefited from sitting around a table with fellow "club members" who had a good idea of what I was saying, thinking, and dealing with.

I want to take a moment here and mention that in each of the two formal groups I attended, and relied on, not all the couples had been married. And not all the relationships had been heterosexual. But each man and each woman was deeply grieving the loss of his or her loved one.

During those early months of my widowhood I discovered a second form of support. This one informal. It was (and is) the widow of one of my cousins and a widow I had known for years as a friend but not a close friend. The first had lost her husband to cancer seven years earlier. The second's had died of ALS ten years before Monica did.

Now both women are dear, dear friends.

Visiting with each on the phone on a regular basis helped me in countless ways.

There may be members of your immediate or extended family, or among your wide circle of friends or acquaintances, who are widowed. You may think they never talk about their loss but, more likely, they've never talked about their loss to you.

We widows and widowers are a cliquish bunch.

Now, sad to say, you're one of them. Or as they, and I, would put it: you're one of us.

And many of us like to help "the new kid." We want to

do that because we know how overwhelming early widowhood can be. And we know how there is no completely "getting over it," no total "closure," but there is learning to live with it.

Starting that conversion with a more experienced widow or widower is pretty easy if the other person wants to talk about it. Something as simple as asking him or her, "What year did _____ die?" Or "Do you remember anything from the funeral?" (Probably only small bits and pieces, if that person is like most of us who are widowed.)

In little or no time, the discussion can open into all kinds of widowhood-related areas. Some, based on my own early-widowhood experience, might include: "What was it like when the body was removed from the house?" "Do you still sleep on 'your' side of the bed?" "How did you pick a headstone and decide what to put on it?"

And, bottom line: "How did you get through it?" "It" being those early days, weeks, month, years.

"Baby steps." "Prayer." "I don't know."

How would I answer that question?

Professional help, those classes and groups led by a social worker.

Family.

And fellow widows and widowers.

Grace of God? Absolutely.

But, I'm convinced, in a large, large way, it was those people—coming formally and informally into my life—who were the conduits of that grace

Holy Spirit, help those who are grieving find the support they need. (Including me!)

20
GETTING ADVICE FROM THOSE WHO KNOW

It's interesting to hear what parental advice children remember from their childhood. My kids sometimes quote "You gotta eat and you gotta sleep." I stressed that after I had written a newspaper series on pseudo-religious cults and learned how poor nutrition and lack of sleep were two of the basic tools used to "convert" potential new members.

It was a long time ago that my own mother told me, "Sometimes we have to do things we don't want to do." As I recall, that centered on a homework assignment but, over the years, I've come to see it applies in many situations.

It's tempting to think the Holy Spirit's gift of wisdom is always delivered in a flash of personal insight. No doubt, sometimes it is. But, as you know, oftentimes it isn't. Instead, it comes from a dad who was freaked out at how easily young people can be manipulated by those who want to take advantage of them. Or by a mom, probably tired of listening to a whining grade-schooler complain about some simple book report (assigned weeks ago and due the next morning), pointing out one of life's basic realities.

Sometimes we're the ones being offered that bit of

wisdom. And, as creatures with free will, we can take it or leave it. Other times we're the ones offering the advice, the ones pointing out a truth, and then we have to accept the fact the person we're trying to help can take it or leave it.

Further complicating all this, sometimes we have that wisdom and know it to be helpful, but we ignore it anyway.

We're no longer a kid but we don't want to eat green vegetables, or shut off the television or computer and get to bed early enough to have a good night's rest. Or we don't even attempt to do what we don't want to do: to acknowledge, to face, and to deal with a situation—a reality—that there's no way around. One that may only get worse if we *don't* acknowledge it, face it, and deal with it.

I reminded myself of that struggle as I went through the third month after Monica' death. *I* have to eat right and get enough sleep. (And get some regular exercise, too.) *I* have to do what I don't want to do. To continue to acknowledge, face, and deal with that reality.

But … .

Because of the wisdom of others, a wisdom that had come through their personal and professional experience, I didn't have to figure out all of this on my own. I didn't have to stumble through that time, any more than the stumbling that can't be avoided because it's a part of grieving.

The same holds true for you and your family, for what you (singular) alone or you (plural) together are facing. God's answer to "Dear Lord, help me!" might be the friend, the book, the counselor, the support group ready to offer years of experience and true knowledge. Any one of them may be God's way of offering you wisdom … and leading you toward peace.

Heavenly Father, give me the strength
to find and use the help I need.

21
RECOGNIZING AND ACCEPTING WHAT YOU CAN AND CAN'T DO

It was early into my widowhood when I started recognizing and accepting the fact there were some things I couldn't do. Not now. At least, not yet.

I wanted to go to Sunday Mass. But, sometimes, I'd drive toward the church, become overwhelmed with grief, and turn around and head for home. Yes, I take my Sunday obligation seriously. Plus, I love the Mass.

But . . . .

I realized the horrid, horrid grief I was experiencing right then could be compared to having a medical problem of another kind. A sudden onset of the stomach flu, for example. Or a high fever. If it had been one of those would I go home and rest?

Of course.

So … was this different? Yes and no. Yes, because from the outside looking in, others probably wouldn't be able to detect what was going on inside me. Except, perhaps, for a serious and distracted look on my face. "And this—what?—some two months or more after his wife had died? Surely, he's come to terms with that by now and moved forward.

Hasn't he?"

You know the answer to that one.

But, no, this *wasn't* different from the flu or fever. With those, I would still want to be at Mass but clearly know I couldn't be. And *shouldn't* be.

For several years Sunday Mass continued to be the hardest regular event for me. (Anniversaries, birthdays, and holidays can be worse, of course.) Monica and I met helping out with babysitting at the University of Washington's Newman Center on Sunday mornings during the first Mass. We'd go together to the second one. Throughout our marriage, we almost always went to Sunday Mass as a couple.

After her death, when I was able to attend Mass, I couldn't sit in "our" pew. And, sometimes, I couldn't stay through the whole Mass. The welling-up of grief was too much to handle there. I would walk out. Get to the car. Cry all the way home.

In my head I could imagine others (non-widows and non-widowers!) counseling, "Oh, no, there's no better place to be with than at Mass with our merciful Lord. Unite your suffering to the suffering at Calvary and … ."

To which my imagined response was: "You don't know what you're talking about." (Which I thought was much more charitable than "Shut up.")

Deep in grief, I couldn't go to Mass. I couldn't make it through Mass.

God knew that. God understood that.

What I could do was offer up that suffering—so much suffering!—as a prayer (what I used to call a "beefy prayer") for the particular intentions and situations of others.

It wasn't the same as going to Mass. But it had some kick to it.

I can think of two other examples of my being unable to do some things. These having to with family gathering. The first was eighteen months after Monica died. My siblings-in-law were gathering in a nearby state to mark their dad's one hundredth birthday. He had passed away three years earlier. I wanted to see them but … it was too much for me. That amount of driving and socializing.

It was beyond what I was able to do.

The second example is one with my own siblings. Four of us live in the Seattle area and my brother, who lives in California, was going to be here for a week in July. We'd all get together several times during that period and one of the events was an all-day excursion to a variety of favorite family spots.

Again, I wanted to go on our "field trip." Again, after planning to take part, I knew I couldn't.

You may have experienced, and will continue to experience, similar situations. Both large and small. The advice I would give myself then, and the one I offer to you now, is this:

Be kind to yourself. Be patient with yourself.

Maybe it helps to think of all this the same way you would a physical injury, one that needs therapy. Sometimes you have to push, and that's doable. Sometimes if you push, if you try to do too much too soon, you set back your recovery or even cause further damage.

Although, of course, "recovery" isn't the right word when it comes to widowhood. In this case, it would be setting back your moving forward for a time as you continue adjusting to your new life.

God knows that, like a twisted knee or broken wrist, grief takes time. How much? As much as needed. And you're the only one who can determine that.

In my own experience, I knew … when I knew. Later, I could go out on an all-day family event. I could go to Sunday Mass, from beginning to end.

Baby steps. (A very common term in this book.) Baby steps on your pilgrimage. "Your" singular.

Please, Lord, help me not feel guilty when there are things I want to do but just can't. Not right now. Not yet.

22
WRITING IT DOWN

On the day after Monica's funeral, alone in our house—my house—I pulled out an old but never used 10½-by-8-inch spiral-bound notebook and wrote:

Wed 1/16/13
MDV – edit May edition
2 mile walk
1½ mile walk (from post office, library, store)

("MDV" meant *My Daily Visitor*, the magazine Monica and I edited. Our part in the process was due many months before the publication date.)

I had no idea why I was jotting down those things. Or what I was doing. Or what it would become.

The next evening I made a list of what I had done *that* day. And the next and the next and the next. Now I'm on my fourth spiral notebook.

Early on I liked it much more than a to-do list. There was so much to do! You know. And so much I didn't want to do or simply couldn't do. Not then. Not on *this* day. You know that, too.

I don't think I ever wrote "sat in a chair in the living room," although that was how I spent a good deal of my time. The television on, making noise, changing images. So I could put "watched TV." I would include "rested" if I lay on the bed. Or "nap," if I had slept. Or "rested and napped," if I lay for a while and then, finally, fell asleep.

Little things that were big things. Hard things. Going to the grocery store. Paying the bills. Filling out a life insurance benefit form. Doing the laundry.

Writing it down in the evening gave me a sense of accomplishment. I needed that. And it helped me remember. I needed that, too.

Oh, this is what I did earlier this week. See? I got some things done.

Oh, this is what I was doing a month ago. Or trying to do but couldn't. I had started driving toward … but burst into tears and had to turn around a go back home.

As the days, weeks, months, and years went by—and, yes, they do go by—I could look back and see what was happening on this day back then. I could notice how I'd made progress and could remember how tough, how horrible, it was in that early period.

This is from one year and one day after Monica's funeral:

Thu 1/16/14
First year over. A long year. Tired.

(And other items. Now I read my two grandchildren spent the next night here with me on January 17th. *That* wouldn't have been possible one year earlier.)

I want to be clear. None of this is to say you should write things down in a similar way. And it certainly doesn't mean you must.

This is what worked, what works, for me.

Another form of writing may be better for you. A journal. A diary. Poems. Prayers. Snippets of what will become a memoir. But maybe the opposite is true. Perhaps any kind of writing and remembering at this point on your pilgrimage would rip you apart inside.

The "right" way for you to grieve, for you to survive that first year, those first years, is *your* way. And a lot of the heavy lifting over that period is figuring out—trial and error, hit and miss—what that way is. For now. A "hit" now might become a "miss" later. An "error" now might become the perfect solution for you at some point in the future.

Heavenly Father, help me find the ways to find my way.

23

"FALLING" INTO WIDOWHOOD

One support group member put it this way: "I was crazy in love, now I'm crazy in grief."

And, he continued, since he had been blessed to have had all that first "crazy"—to receive her love and give his in return—he could accept the second "crazy."

If their love for each other hadn't been so huge early in their relationship and throughout their marriage, his grief wouldn't be as deep as it was now. The vastness of the pain reflected the vastness of the joy.

While every married couple's relationship is unique, for most of us, falling in love was overwhelming. It colored our life in so many wonderful ways. Touched not just our heart, but our mind and our soul.

That love could influence how you felt, how you thought, and even how you prayed.

You wanted to spend your life with him or her. Now you can't imagine the rest of your life without that person. You don't want to imagine it. The thought is more than bleak, it's terrifying.

You had wanted to rush into the future with him or with her. To glide through it, together. Now just thinking about getting through a day is more than you can stand.

A morning. An afternoon. An evening. A night.

O, Dear Lord, the nights.

And then you wake—or simply give up on trying to sleep—and get up to face another day. One more morning. Afternoon. Evening. And night.

Without her. Without him.

The life the two of you imagined, the life the two of you built for and with each other, is so radically and abruptly changed because his life, because her life, is gone.

But that's not entirely true.

Your loved one's life isn't completely gone. In the words of the Catholic funeral rite: "life is changed, not ended."

There can be comfort in that. Knowing a soul is eternal. Knowing that a couple's love continues—both ways—even after a husband or wife dies.

But!

What no one tells you, what no homilist at a funeral mentions, is that *your* life has changed … not ended.

Now, with time, with prayer, with effort and perseverance, your life continues. And part of that includes discovering what that new life is.

There's no timeline. There's no being able to rush through it to get it "done" faster. No gliding.

Your new life will come. Piece by piece you'll discover bits of peace. Moments of joy. A sense of calm.

But for now, especially in those first days, weeks, months, and sometimes years, it helps tremendously if that new life includes being patient with yourself. Being kind to yourself. (I say that often in this book because longtime widows and widowers said it often to me.)

It's what you would want for your spouse if you had died first and she was now a widow. If he was now a widower.

It's what your dear one wants for you.

It's what God wants for you.

It will come.

That peace, that joy, that calm will come.

A sense of purpose will come as this new stage of your life continues to unfold at its own pace and in its own way.

There's no "falling" into it.

But it will come.

Just for now, Holy Spirit, ease my pain.
Bring me a moment of peace.

24
"YOU'RE GRIEVING WRONG"

I found it helpful to keep in mind—and to mention to my fellow widows and widowers gathered around a table at a support group meeting— that some people … .

I hesitate to say "are morons" but I think I'm accurate in saying "act moronically." People who are, to put it bluntly, stupid and insensitive.

Yes, yes, love your neighbor as you love yourself, and love your enemy, but … don't argue with fools. They say things that are hurtful or even harmful.

This is something you may have come up against a time or two. Or three.

One example that comes to mind is a widow who was a special education teacher. Not long after her husband died of cancer (she was forty-seven, he was fifty-three), a fellow faculty member let her know, "You're grieving wrong."

She was devastated. And felt guilty. Perhaps the reason she was feeling so horrible and having such an extremely hard time was because she *was* grieving "wrong." But … what was the right way?

Being very kind-hearted, she invited the fellow teacher to her house so they could talk about it. There, she listened for a time, and then her colleague left. Perhaps (and it seems likely) the visitor was pleased at being able to straighten out this recent widow.

A good deed done.

Almost a decade later, when the teacher told me this story, I asked her, "Had the other teacher lost her husband?"

No.

"Did she have some experience of deep grief after losing a loved one?"

No.

"But she knew more about grieving than you did and knew you were grieving 'wrong'?"

Yes.

Hmm.

Among the many ways our defenses are down in that early widowhood period is our ability to recognize … I hesitate to use the words "an idiot" so I'll say "someone who is acting idiotically."

If we weren't so exhausted, stressed, and overwhelmed in so many, many ways, it would be easier to recognize that kind of behavior for what it is and be easier to deal with it. To defend ourselves against it. To run from it.

In a similar way that when we're tired, stressed, or haven't been eating properly, our bodies are more susceptible to catching a cold, the flu, or some other illness, entering widowhood our emotional immune system is on the fritz.

I've found, as a widower, it's been helpful for me to ask myself:

- Does this person offering advice or opinions know anything about widowhood? Or even grief in general?
- Does what he or she is saying sound like something that will help me or just add more work, more stress?

Complicating this is sometimes the person offering "help" does it with the best of intentions and, at other times, it's just a busybody or know-it-all.

And among the "advice" they offer is:

- "You have to force yourself to get up and get going to feel better."
- "You're going to be fine once you get through that first year."
- "Just try something new. You're lucky you have so much free time."
- "Finish going through the stages of grief and you'll find closure."
- "It's time you quit moping around."

And on and on.

But none of those advisors—well-meaning or not—is on the path you're on. The pilgrimage you're on.

None of them had a spouse like your spouse. A marriage like your marriage. A life like your life.

At times, being kind to yourself means protecting yourself.

Heavenly Father, protect me from those who mean well but don't know what they're talking about, or who are just bossy, and give me the strength to make it through today.

25
MAKING DECISIONS

It's not surprising decisions can be hard to make after the death of your spouse. But then again, you may be surprised to discover you *are* having a hard time with them.

It's *not* surprising because just about everything is hard in early widowhood. (Except crying. I became a real champ at that.)

And it *is* surprising because you probably had no idea how much you relied on your dear one to offer advice or give an opinion. (Sometimes whether or not you wanted it.)

Often, that advice or opinion was one you valued. He or she was a sounding board you trusted. Then, too, sometimes it was a joint decision. Not a (grumble, grumble) compromise, but a decision that you both liked more than either's original idea.

Having to decide—alone—can be so terribly hard at a time when you've been shaken to your core. You may have heard the advice not to make any big decisions during the first year of widowhood. (As one longtime widow pointed out to me as my own one-year anniversary drew closer, "You can always extend it for another year.")

I like that one. I know it helped me, including getting out

of some things I didn't want to do. But I didn't have to make any big choices. I didn't need to sell my house. To move to be closer to the children or another family member. To go back to work because now finances were tight.

I know that's not always the case. And I know widows and widowers who have successfully made big changes like that during their first year.

Still … .

Day in and day out, all those days can seem peppered (plagued!) with having to make decisions. From what to eat to what to put on your spouse's headstone.

I use that as an example because I was slow, slow, slow in getting Monica's. It took me two years. Until then, I just wasn't ready. Even then, I had a bit of … "headstone-buyer's remorse"?

It wasn't as if I stewed about it every day but it was something that would surface and I'd push aside for another few months. I had asked my two trusted widowed advisors and, in this case, neither was much help.

One's husband had been cremated and the ashes dispersed. The other said she hadn't been able to make that decision and so, very early, had told the cemetery staff to just pick something.

On a much lighter note here, there was a widow in my group who reported she was at a department store and couldn't decide between two pairs of shoes. "I went back and forth for quite a while and then I just said, 'To hell with it. I'll buy both pairs and take one pair back later.'"

We congratulated her on her problem-solving skills.

There *was* one big decision I made in the late days of Monica's illness and the early days of my widowhood: I chose to have faith in God. I remember that vividly. Saying, praying, "I *choose* to have faith in you."

And he, I see now, had faith in me. Together, we would go through, get through, Monica's dying and that horrid early period of immense grief.

Holy Spirit, give me the wisdom to make good decisions and to trust myself more.

26

STRESS RAMPED UP TO 11 ON A SCALE OF 1 TO 10

I remember reading that having a spouse die is the most stressful event a person can go through. After Monica passed away I thought, "I sure hope so."

You know what I mean although, I suspect, neither of us can fully and accurately describe it. "It's like this … only much, much more. Much, much worse."

One support group member in his eighties who was having a really hard time sleeping—and, after seeing his doctor, began taking medicine to help with that—said: "I was in the Korean War and that was *nothing* compared to this." (He didn't say if he had been in combat.)

I suppose I shouldn't have been surprised that the stress was so extreme. The death of your husband or wife is overwhelming in a lot of ways, many of them overlapping and piling one on top of the other in that early period of widowhood.

I was fortunate—blessed—to have had Monica's hospice social worker pay me a visit a little while after Monica had died. One of the topics she covered was the stress of early grief.

In the days that followed I recognized some of the typical symptoms of hyper-stress when I began having them. Some were mental. Confusion. Having trouble coming up with a word, for example. And some were physical. I couldn't hold a cup of coffee without spilling it. I had to use a mug, no more than half filled.

The one I found the strangest was an inability to focus on one task and complete it. Not a big task by any means. Something like putting the cordless phone back into its charging cradle. Just walking from one room to another to do that I could get diverted. Oh, I should get the hamper out to the washing machine. Oh, look at the grime that's built up on the top of the washing machine. I should wipe that down. Oh, well, as long as I'm doing a little cleaning I should … .

I didn't know if there was such a thing as "temporary attention deficit disorder" but, it seemed to me, that was what I had.

Early on, one way I dealt with that stress was overeating. Junk food. Chocolate! Not the best solution. Not the worst. As one widower in our group said, "I started drinking more. Just a little bit each day. Pretty soon I had *two* problems." We nodded. Many of us had done that one way or another.

Walking helped me. It filled up time. Made me tired. And somehow burned away feelings of anxiety and kept them from overwhelming me later that day.

Another big stress reliever was talking to fellow widows and widowers. Sometimes in a group, sometime one-on-one with a widowhood "veteran." I remember—referring to an anti-anxiety medication that Monica took as needed during the last half year of her life—saying to one friend, "You're better than lorazepam."

She was.

But, of course, just like your widowhood, your stress is yours. It's unique. One-of-a-kind. And so, too, are the best ways for you to handle it. To come to learn to handle it.

And, at times, just live with it.

Prince of (Inner) Peace, be with me now.

27
THE CHARACTERISTICS OF GRIEF

At one support group meeting we were given a list similar to this one. I have no doubt most, if not all, of us could check off at least half of the items.

And, often, they overlapped. They came and went. Over time, they lessened and some disappeared. Perhaps not forever, but at least for a time.

For a very welcome time.

- Feeling confused, forgetful, disorganized, or thinking more slowly than unusual.
- An inability to concentrate or pay attention.
- To forget what you were going to do, not finish what you began, or just wander.
- Over and over, to repeat and remember things about your spouse and their death.
- To feel that somehow the loss isn't real, that it never happened.
- To sense the presence of your spouse, expect them to walk into the room just as they always did.

- A feeling of numbness, tightness in the throat, heaviness in the chest, or sense of unreality. A dazed or "out of body" experience.
- Swift changes in mood.
- Wanting to be alone, wanting not to be alone.
- Wanting to avoid feelings because they're intense.
- Feeling that life has lost its meaning.
- Thoughts of suicide.
- Sadness, fear, anger. Sometimes strongly felt. And, at times, perhaps a feeling of relief, or simultaneous and contradictory attitudes or feelings.
- Guilt or anger at what did or didn't happen in the marriage. Feelings of rejection or loneliness.
- Crying frequently, deeply, or unexpectedly.
- An inability to take pleasure in things, including those that used to be fun.
- Being very angry that they left you.
- Changes in appetite. Eating more, or less, with accompanying weight gain or loss.
- Chest pains, abdominal pains, headaches, or nausea. Susceptibility to illness.
- Constant fatigue. Unable to sleep or wanting to sleep all the time.
- To dream of your loved one frequently.
- Feeling restless or agitated.
- Clumsiness, being more prone to accidents
- Avoiding talking about your spouse or loss so others aren't uncomfortable.

Yes, grief is filled with stress but stress doesn't always include grief nor, in particular instances, is it the cause of it. Stress at work, for example, or financial concerns.

That's why dealing with the characteristics of grief, and the forms of stress that are a part of grief, isn't identical to handling work or money stress.

Still, some basics apply to both: taking care of yourself, being patient with yourself, being kind to yourself. Getting help from professionals if needed, as well as from others.

The more you learn about the characteristics of grief the easier it is to recognize them in your life now. And, that too, can help lower your stress level.

In many ways, the symptoms of this horrible, overwhelming, and abnormal period are perfectly normal for one who's grieving.

For you, a widow or widower.

Walk with me, Dear Jesus, as I stumble and bumble through this time. Help me hang on to you.

28
GUILT AND FORGIVENESS

During Monica's final months, when we knew she had less than a year to live, something I had done or had failed to do would pop into my head.

As awful as it was knowing she was going to die too soon, it did give me an opportunity not just to say "I love you" more often but also "I'm sorry."

I'm sorry I was such a stinker when it came to your buying me gifts. (At one point she gave up and told me to buy whatever I *really* wanted and that was from her.)

I'm sorry I made us walk out of so many restaurants after I saw the prices on the menu.

I'm sorry … I'm sorry … I'm sorry.

There are still events or choices or actions in our relationship that I feel guilty about. That I'm sorry for. But during those final months, Monica fell into a pattern of answering my apology in one of three ways:

1."I don't even remember that."

2. "Oh, you can let that go."

3. "That was a tough one."

I still think about those. And I've shared the list with others widows and widowers, especially those whose spouse died suddenly and unexpectedly.

If their loved one had had the opportunity to offer forgiveness, and if he or she could have known how hard widowhood is for you, then—no doubt—you would have heard one of those three responses.

In one way or another.

I suppose you're like me and wish you could have been a better spouse. Neither Monica nor I could have been perfect. But it would have been nice to be *better.* If I just could have been better.

Being very certain Monica would have offered me one of those three responses helps but sometimes, I confess, it doesn't seem to be enough. That's when I imagine her saying to me, "Think about all you did that was right. That was helpful. That was loving. That was … *you.*"

Then my thoughts slip to ways I was a good husband. Times when I offered the support, the comfort, and the love that was mine alone, uniquely mine, to give her.

And then I remember when she did the same for me. Again and again. Throughout the many years of our married life. (But not enough years!)

Thank you, Dear Lord, for the ability to ask for forgiveness, to forgive, and to accept forgiveness. And thank you for the sacrament of reconciliation.

29
WIDOWHOOD'S "HAPPINESS GUILT"

Among the many cruelties of widowhood is feeling bad when, miracle of miracles, you start to feel good. That little glimmer of sunlight. That inkling of joy. That one, deep breath of peace. Each a betrayal!

Or so it may seem.

How can I be happy, if only for a moment or two, when my loved one … ?

The mantle of widowhood, like a chainmail overcoat, is a tremendous burden. You know that. It can crush you throughout the day and well into the night until, at last, completely exhausted, you fall into a restless sleep.

If a sliver of sunlight, joy, or peace happens, does that mean you're betraying your loved one? That you're beginning to forget about him or her? That your love is growing weaker? You don't want to betray, forget, or let that love lessen.

Of course you don't. And you're not.

Sometimes it helps me to "flip" the situation. To imagine I was the one who had died and it was Monica who now felt a little joy or peace. What would my reaction be? "You're forgetting me! How dare you!" Not likely. I'd want for her what I'd always wanted for her. Joy, peace, and love. A happy, healthy, holy life.

And what if you had been the one who died? Now, realizing how much your spouse cared for you, how deeply he or she loved you, how much grief, how much suffering your death has brought … . I bet you'd be so pleased that your beloved felt a little happiness. You'd be delighted! Thrilled! It's what you'd want for your spouse, and not just a little joy but a ton of joy. Of peace. Of rest.

It seems safe to speculate that's what your dear departed one, your honey, wants for you.

"Moving on" doesn't mean abandoning. Your spouse moves with you. Walking ahead and gently leading you forward. Standing behind and giving you a solid push when you need it. Often walking next to you, with you.

Just as during all the years of your marriage.

Not in the same way. Not in a way you or I or anyone on earth can understand. But it happens. Your love for him or her, his or hers love for you, didn't end with death. Death took a life but not the love two souls shared then and share now. That's a big part of what the Communion of Saints is all about. Those who have died can help those of us still here.

In heaven, they have complete and eternal joy. On earth, we still have a rocky, crooked, uphill way to go. A way that, you know, can include such overwhelming sorrow.

But, widows and widowers come to discover, it can still have joy. And peace.

And indescribable love.

Those first glimmers of sunlight and inklings of joy are signs of your healing. Heart, mind, and soul. But they don't lead to a wholeness that's perfectly matches what you had before you become a member of "the club."

They're (baby!) steps toward a wholeness that includes new forms of happiness … and holiness. New forms that, for some, may move us to dating or marriage. For others, to new kinds of service to those in need. To new vocations or careers. To new interests and friends. To new graces and blessings.

And to new challenges, including continuing along your pilgrimage with grief growing smaller and smaller but never completely gone because it can still flare up at times.

They're part of the path on your pilgrimage that will end with your being united with God.

And reunited with your sweetie pie.

Forever and ever. Amen.

Thank you, Lord, for moments of happiness. Help me see each one as a gift from my dear ______________, as something sent special delivery … and sealed with a kiss.

30

"IF ONLY" GUILT

I suspect that just about every widow and widower experiences at least a twinge of "if only" guilt for a number of reasons.

First, no matter the circumstances, it can seem that somehow and someway that death was at least partly "my" fault.

If only I had done this … if only I hadn't done that … then … .

She would have gone to the doctor and started treatment sooner.

He would have been better about taking care of himself.

She wouldn't have been in that car.

He wouldn't have been alone when … .

Sometimes that guilt is misplaced, but it's hard to see it that way. Other times it's somewhat accurate and becomes part of the crushing burden of early widowhood. A part that, with time, lessens.

It can be helpful to recognize and remember that most often we do the best we can with the information—and wisdom—we have at the time. Now, we would do things differently. But then … .

Coupled with that is the truth that most often, almost always, a small action has only a small consequence. A husband and wife argue and one storms out for a walk. But comes back. Fine. Cooled off. Both apologize.

Or a couple goes for a meandering drive on a Sunday afternoon. At a fork in the road, one asks "Which way?" and the other answers "Left." The drive continues. A pleasant outing.

A little spat. A Sunday outing. A normal event, like so many others that are a part of marriage. But if, somehow, the cooling-off period or the choosing of that left fork ends with … .

Death. Widowhood. You here and now.

It's a scene, a choice, a decision the one who's left behind can replay a thousand times in his or her head. With an undertone of: Through my fault. Through my fault. Through my most grievous fault.

From the Confiteor, right? But continue that prayer:

Therefore I ask blessed Mary ever-Virgin,
all the Angels and Saints,
and you, my brothers and sisters,
to pray for me to the Lord our God.

Then, at Mass, it's the priest who continues:

May almighty God have mercy on us,
forgive us our sins,
and bring us to everlasting life.

Bring you—imperfect you—to your spouse. To an everlasting life together. Amen

Dear Lord, forgive me for what I have done and what I have failed to do. Dear Lord, help me forgive myself.

31
EXHAUSTION

Of course you're exhausted. Grief saps energy in so many ways. Physically, mentally, emotionally, spiritually, psychologically … . The list goes on and on. Death took your loved one's life and sorrow sucks the life out of you.

Day by day. Night by night. For a time, but not forever. A body, mind, heart, and soul can regain strength. With time. With patience. With an amount of effort that's appropriate—that's just right—for you.

Which is … what? No one knows. Not even you, starting out on your pilgrimage. How much rest? How many tears? How many days, weeks, months, years?

I noticed among new group members that some became widowed after many years of being a frontline caregiver. And some found themselves at the table after their spouse passed away suddenly and unexpectedly.

Having worked in a ministry to caregivers for a long time, I liked to tell those who had lost a spouse after a lengthy illness that "Of course you're exhausted. Even if your loved one had miraculously been completely healed you would still be very, very tired for a long time. Instead, when you were on the brink, or over the brink, from all your caregiving duties, now you're face-to-face with the loss of your spouse. With *huge* grief."

A new exhaustion on top of an old. A familiar exhaustion coupled with one that's unknown.

And what about those whose spouse's death came … out of the blue? For them there was no preparing. Often, there was no saying "Goodbye." No "I love you." Yes, that and more is said now but not to him, not to her, at that final moment. Or at least near that final moment.

When other widows and widowers spoke of that it was clear it weighed heavily on their hearts and minds. And on their bodies.

(That's one of the advantages of speaking to fellow widows and widowers who have a variety of experiences of a spouse's death. Some, similar to yours. Others, very different. Each brings a perspective not just of the circumstances of the death, but of the particular challenges of the grieving.)

I never, ever, heard a recent widow or widower speak of feeling rested and ready to go. It took time, and self-care, to deal with initial grief's exhaustion. For some that included individual counseling or therapy, and a doctor prescribing the appropriate medication.

I'm sure that for all of us it meant going slow, accepting we *had* to go slow because that was our only choice. It meant doing less, resting more, and being patient with, and kind to, ourselves.

Heavenly Father, help me rest. Help me sleep. Help me.

32
MAKING A PLAN FOR AN IMPORTANT DAY

I still follow a piece of advice I received some six months into my widowhood: make a plan for an important day.

For your spouse's or your birthday. For an anniversary or a holiday. And so on.

Then, too, there can be "private anniversaries." Dates most other people wouldn't know or remember. The day you met. A first kiss. The day you got engaged. The day you received the horrible diagnosis. And others.

What could a "plan" be? Going to Mass (or having a Mass said for him or her). Visiting the cemetery or a place you two frequented. Having a meal out or eating something special at home. Perhaps as much as doing some traveling. Going away for a few days or more. (Many widows and widowers "take off" for Christmas.)

It can help a lot to have someone else included in your plan. Someone who supports you in your grief. Someone who doesn't add to your troubles. Who knows how to listen, when to speak, and when to be silent. (Those friends and family members are more precious than gold!)

All that being said, when that day arrives you may not

want to do any of it. You may be incapable of doing any of it. That's OK. For you, at that point in your grief, what may be best, most healthy in many ways, is a quiet day of rest.

That's been true for me. As I had been advised, and as I've found to be true, sometimes a part of what mattered was just having the plan in place.

Over my years of widowhood I've discovered that what one veteran widow told me early on is very true. Sometimes the time building up to a particular, important day is harder than the day itself. That day isn't as bad as I thought it would be.

In recent years I've also come to notice that sometimes I'm not aware of feelings of grief slowly surfacing as the day approaches. It's as if my heart and body know the day is closing in on me. Subconsciously, it's weighing heavy on my mind. I find myself sadder, more tired, unable to get things done, and even a little weepy, and I can't figure out why.

And then it occurs to me. Of course!

I can make a plan. Or, knowing why I'm going to be upset for a time, just accept it. It's never pleasant but it's not the overwhelming and sometimes debilitating emotions of early grief.

Looking back I see that I've developed a tradition to mark the day of Monica's death. Her sister, my daughter, and I go out to lunch. There we enjoy each other's company as we tell favorite "Monica stories" and sometimes come up with some new ones. There, three people who loved her so dearly, share that love with each other.

And in a wonderful, inexplicable way, somehow she's with us.

Oh, Dear Holy Spirit, how I dread some upcoming birthdays, anniversaries, and holidays. Be with me, be with me, be with me.

33
GETTING THAT FIRST CHECK-UP AFTER YOUR SPOUSE DIES

I kept reading about how it was a good idea to visit your primary care physician after your spouse died. To get a physical examination because grief can do so much to your body and your mind.

I suppose I decided to go because, I was sure, Monica would want me to do that. It was important. I needed to take care of myself for my sake and, more importantly, for the sake of my kids and grandkids.

Then, too, I had started making a list of problems I seemed to be having. This hurt, that didn't seem normal, and on and on. About a dozen symptoms, eight of which, I was sure, were terminal.

A grim outcome from a small concern now seemed very possible. Wasn't that what had happened to Monica? To her doctor, to a specialist, to surgery, to chemotherapy, to radiation and … to death. (Yes, over almost three years, but the sequence was there.)

Fortunately (thanks be to God), my doctor was very good. Before he even began the exam he asked if I had any specific concerns. I pulled out my list and we went over them one by one. He calmed my fears one by one.

No, I didn't have this or that or the other.

"Now," he said, "let's take your blood pressure again." The initial reading, taken by a medical assistant before the doctor arrived, had been a little high. This time, it was just fine. The doctor smiled and nodded. Not surprised.

He checked me over from stem to stern and pronounced me healthy. Later, lab work came back with the same results.

What a difference that made. Healthy! One concern on the list of early widowhood's many worries taken care of. (And, of course, if something had needed medical attention, it would have been better to get to it early.)

"You can come back in a few months," the doctor said when he was done with the exam.

"Why … ?"

He could tell his offer confused me. "If you'd like to talk," he said. That meant the world to me. I told him I was attending a class on widowhood. That I was able to talk, listen, and learn there.

It was at a support group meeting a few months later that one woman joked, "Widowhood means you wake up in the middle of the night with a cramp in your leg and you're sure it's stage four cancer."

We laughed. Yes, that feeling of alarm still tended to be our first response, too. And, we agreed, finding the healthy and proper balance between overreacting and underreacting was important.

I don't blame you if you're hesitant to get a check-up. We like to think no news is *always* good news, even though we know that's not true.

My going in for that first exam after Monica died was very stressful. My coming out about forty-five minutes later was so very, very peaceful.

One of the ways I gathered up my courage to make the appointment, show up for it, and hide none of my concerns from the doctor, was "flipping" my situation. (A strategy

I've mentioned earlier.) That may help you, too. I thought about what I would want Monica to do if I had been the one who died.

I'd want her to get the exam. I'd want her to take care of herself.

I'd want her to join me in the next life … but not yet. Not till it was her time, on God's schedule, for us to be back together. No shortcuts!

Dear Lord, help me take care of myself, especially when I'm afraid to do that.

34
STARTING LENT AFTER THE DEATH OF YOUR LOVED ONE

Lent has a way of sneaking up on all of us each year. That can be especially so if you've recently lost a loved one.

On my first Ash Wednesday after Monica died I was determined to get to Mass and receive the ashes on my forehead. But as I drove closer to church, thoughts of the annual reminder "Remember, you are dust and to dust you will return" were just too much for me.

I drove to the cemetery where Monica is buried and prayed there. Cried there.

Later that morning I was still wishing I had been able to get to Mass and receive the ashes when I headed to the combination assisted-living facility/nursing home where Monica's mother and my mom lived. I made that weekly visit … when I was able.

(My mother-in-law, Terry Faudree, died in early May of that year. My mom passed away at the end of May. My children lost their mother and both grandmothers within five months.)

As I stepped out of the elevator on the nursing home floor where my mother was receiving care, the chaplain—a dear nun—gave me a big, smudgy thumbs up from down the hallway. She was distributing ashes to the residents. Would I like to receive them?

I was close to tears, by now a familiar sensation.

Yes!

And to receive Holy Communion?

Yes, yes, yes!

I realized that on a day when I couldn't get to church and to Our Lord in the Eucharist, Christ and his church came to me.

I went on to have lunch with my mom and to spend some time with my mother-in-law in her apartment.

And then …

I detoured on my way home, stopped at an electronics store, and bought a PlayStation 3 video-game player.

I started that Lent with a new toy. Something that was out of keeping with the penitential season, a little silly for someone my age, out of character for me … and a wonderful distraction. A way to call a "time out" from the overwhelming thoughts, emotions, and necessary tasks associated with the death of a spouse.

Those forty day of Lent were, without a doubt, a time of prayer and a time of reflection on life and death. But they were also a period of long walks, grief-support group meetings, and hours playing video games. (Again and again saving the world from space aliens or earthly monsters!)

It was how I got from "just" thirty-five days after Monica' deaths to a whopping seventy-five days after it. A challenge that, at the time, seemed completely impossible.

I'm telling this story for those who would like to mark this Lent as they have in the past but … just can't.

God knows.

God understands.

God is with you. Right here. Right now.

Be kind to yourself. Be patient.

And, sometimes, be pleasantly surprised.

That first Ash Wednesday after Monica's death was on February 13. The following day was my first Valentine's Day without her in forty years. I couldn't shake the feeling that somehow, someway, that video-game console was a gift from her.

The thought still makes me laugh.

Heavenly Father, help me mark this Lent with the gentle and loving ways you're calling me to do that. Help me avoid getting caught up in my own ideas of what "I should" be doing over these forty days.

35
WHAT HAVE I DONE FOR MY GRIEF TODAY?

After I had been a widower for a while, probably four or five months, I decided it might be a good idea to more deliberately "work on" my grief.

Nothing major. I couldn't do that.

Nothing that would "fix the problem." Not possible.

But something—or a lot a somethings, a daily something—that would help me. Anything, Dear Lord, that would help me.

I remembered a challenging question used by ForYourMarriage.org. Their "What have you done for your marriage today?" became my "What have I done for my grief today?"

Just one thing, I figured. Large or small. But one thing. Large would be going to a support group meeting. When the time came I never wanted to go. Driving there, I wanted to turn around. Later, driving home, I was always so glad and so grateful that I had been able to be there. I always felt better. Tired, but better.

And as for a small thing? Could have been an extra nap. One in the morning *and* in the afternoon. You know how exhausting grief is and a little more, a little extra, sack time truly is one way to help deal with it.

Some days I walked a little bit farther than I usually did. Some days I went to daily Mass or visited the adoration chapel. Some days I picked up dinner at a fast-food place. Some days I went out and had lunch with a friend and some days I stayed home.

Again, you know how that is. The need to socialize and the need to just be alone.

Now, looking back, I can see that it takes time, it takes the experience of that early grieving period, to recognize what it is you need. And to allow yourself to have it. (With practice, that can get to be guilt-free.)

On some days it was reading a little bit about widowhood and grief on a website or in a book. And—be kind to yourself—if the website or book wasn't helpful to me right then and there I'd stop. I didn't need more pressure on "how to grieve" or any … lamebrain … theories on it. Or ones that clashed with my core values and beliefs. *Our* core values and beliefs, the ones Monica and I shared.

Any advice about widowhood you hear or read (including all the material in this book) is just that: only advice. Some won't be a good fit for you. Some you may try and discover for yourself if it's a hit or a miss. Some you may already be doing. And some … some is just not good. (Anyone can write a book, put up a website, or post to sites about widowhood grief.)

But it can help to have information about what other "club members" did or are doing. It can be comforting to learn more about the process of grieving and living with grief after the death of a spouse from solid professionals who have worked in the field for many years.

Big or little, those actions or activities helped me. Each, no matter how small, gave me a feeling of accomplishment. Each, day by day, was a choice not a must-do.

Some days I forgot all about doing one. Some days, I did more than one. I didn't keep score or try to balance out days and deeds.

I have no idea when I stopped deliberately doing "what have I done today" items. It just faded. I don't think it was because I was neglectful. It was just time to move on when it came to that way of dealing with my grief. I suppose—without my being aware of it—my mind, heart, and soul made the decision without me.

They knew. And they were right.

Holy Spirit, help me work on my grief in the ways and at the pace that are best for me.

36
A "THIRD WHEEL": YOUR NEW LIFE IN THE MARGIN

"But from the beginning of creation, 'God made them male and female. For this reason a man shall leave his father and mother [and be joined to his wife], and the two shall become one flesh"' (Mk 10:6-8).

That passage from Mark can hit home, can hit hard, if you're recently widowed.

"The two shall become one." Yes, in flesh, but more than that. One in so many ways you may not have been consciously aware of until the two—you two—were ripped apart.

One of the (many, many) consequences of that is your friends and other married couples may see you differently. And, sometimes, even look at you suspiciously.

As one widower said to me, "People always thought of us as "'BobAndSheila.' One word. One … entity. That's how close we were. That's how much we did things together."

Then he became Bob. Just Bob. Bob, singular. Single Bob.

He didn't tell me if he felt somehow excluded because of

his new status in life as a widower. But it wasn't uncommon for widows in my support group to talk about no longer being invited to gatherings, to parties, to dinners. Those events, they said, tended to be "couples only" and … .

Why, they wondered, were they no longer on the guest list? Why had they lost not only their spouse but their friends, too? Was becoming a widow or widower somehow "socially unacceptable"?

(I never experienced that, but then Monica and I weren't ones to go to dinners and such. Our closest friends, pretty much our only friends, were family members. Plus, we tended to be homebodies.)

When the topic was raised at a support group meeting, several women offered possible reasons for it happening. Among the first was other wives now saw the new widow as some sort of threat to her own marriage.

"As if I were interested in one of *their* husbands!" one said. Then added, "As if, right now, I were interested in dating or getting remarried."

Another theory was the couples didn't want a new widow among them because, so recently, she *had been* one of them: part of a married couple. If it happened to her and her spouse, it could happen to each of them. Her presence now wasn't exactly bad luck, but a grim reminder.

And then, for those at the social gathering, there was the problem of what do you say to that widow or widower? Better to tiptoe around "all that" so the one who's grieving doesn't begin to cry. (There's a party-stopper.) Plus, hasn't it been a while? Couple of months. No reason to bring it up after all this time. Why raise the topic of death during what's supposed to be a pleasant evening?

You know there can be more to this exclusion, don't you? Yes, widowhood can also make you see your parish in a new light. Or at least from a different angle. For good or bad, it's not uncommon for a parish to put its primary focus on families with children, then married couples, and then …

others. Single people, the divorced, and the widowed.

If that's not actually the case, at times it can seem as if it is. Feel as if it is.

It could be, that with the death of your spouse, you've been slid to the margins.

How do you deal with that? Once again, it takes time to grow more accustomed to being in that situation or category. To finding yourself outside the mainstream of your past social life and parish niche, and letting your new ones unfold. It could be you'll discover that many of "your"—plural—friends were really "his" friends or "her" friends. And no longer socializing with them is OK. It could be one of the ways the Holy Spirit offers comfort is by gently moving you toward a different role at the parish. With different blessings and graces.

One more item the widows at my group mentioned: Some kind-hearted, well-meaning friends assume you're not ready for a dinner party or going to a movie or … . And so they don't call, email, or text. They don't ask. They don't invite.

"*You* can do the asking or inviting," one widow said. "You can get in touch with a friend and suggest you meet for coffee or take a walk together. They may want to do that—they miss you and are worried about you—but they just aren't sure how or when to approach you."

(For more on this see Appendix 3: A Handout Sheet to Share with Family and Friends: "A Few Things I Would Like You to Know about Widowhood.")

And, of course, a dear friend, a true friend, will understand if, at the last minute, you just can't meet or walk. That's a friendship worth keeping, fostering, and thanking God for.

But wait there's more! (I sound like an infomercial here.) You may discover new friends, dear friends, friends who *really* understand widowhood because they're widows or widowers. They may be in the parish "margins," in the neighborhood, at work, in your extended family, among former classmates, or part of your own loss support group.

Lord, help the friendships that are important to me continue and grow deeper. And maybe let me make some new, dear friends, too.

37
A NEW KIND OF SINGLE

I was fortunate I had time to prepare for my widowhood but I don't recall it occurring to me that I was going to become a single parent and grandparent.

A dad *and* a mom. A grandpa *and* a grandma.

"Mom and Dad's house" became "Dad's house." "Grandma and Grandpa's house" became "Grandpa's house." Over time. Not right away. In that early period it was just too hard, too much, for my kids or grandkids to make that change. Accept that change. Let that change become a part of the awful reality in which we found ourselves living.

It was a small obstacle compared to so many others that had to be dealt with, but those early times of widowhood are filled with, packed with, "small" obstacles. Changes. Adjustments. Acceptances.

It wasn't that I was going to become Mom or Grandma. It wasn't that I could replace what Monica did and how she did it in each of those roles that were so precious to her and so appreciated by the kids and grandkids.

It was the realization of some of the parenting and grandparenting that was now missing in their lives. It was my trying to figure out how I could do more, could shift my own parenting and grandparenting to help my dear family with their loss.

I hug more now. Kiss goodbye more. Listen more. Talk more.

I suppose, as with so many areas that are divided between a husband and wife, a dad and mom, a grandfather and grandmother, the division of labor, of assignments, just fell into place over the years. A good division. One that worked well.

One plus one equals two, but in a happy marriage, one plus one can add up to a new, fantastic, and truly blessed new *one*. A one made up of, made up by, both of you.

Widowhood means a new "one," a single "one." But it's not the one you were before you were married. As you know, it's not like going back to a somewhat familiar square one. Suddenly, often unexpectedly, most often horribly, a widow or widower is on a *new* square one.

Part of it is assuming the mantle, to one degree or another, of the many roles that were included in your spouse's share of the division of labor and the division of love (The unique way he or she lived out his or her relationship with children and grandchildren and with other loved ones.)

And part of the widowhood challenge now is beginning to figure out who you *are* now. What you like and what you don't like. What you enjoy and don't enjoy. What new things you want to try and old things you choose to drop.

For me, none of this was immediate. This sorting, sifting, and shifting didn't start to happen until months and months after Monica died. It was, and is, gradual. Small decisions. Small changes. (Which, sometimes, I quickly "unchanged." Rearrange the living room furniture? Why not? Do it, look at it, and immediately move it back to the way it had been. That took me an hour one morning.)

It can help to remember if the "new you" makes a

change it isn't a betrayal of your spouse. And if you keep something the way it was (still go the nine o'clock Mass on Sunday, still have Friday as laundry day, still look forward to "our" television program on Tuesday night) it doesn't mean you're somehow stuck in the past and need to move on with your life.

Your life is moving on, with or without your approval. And, in some areas, you get to choose how it moves on … or stays put.

Your life. Your widowhood. Your pilgrimage.

I'm glad you never change, God. I love you just the way you are.
(Even if you can be so hard to understand!)

38
YOUR CHANGING INTERESTS AND PLEASURES

It could be something you used to like to do no longer brings you any pleasure. And, after a time, you may discover comfort and happiness in doing something new you never thought you'd do.

It wasn't until after Monica died that I realized what was going on with my mom who, after being a widow a while, became a baseball fan. She'd watch the Seattle Mariners on television and listen to the TV broadcasts after her eyesight failed.

She knew the players and their stories and would happily visit on the phone with a fellow widow friend who also enjoyed the game.

Dad had been a baseball fan (though no fanatic) but I don't remember him and Mom watching games together. Perhaps, on some level, her watching them after his death helped her feel close to him. But maybe not. It could just be she tried a broadcast or two and then tried a couple more. Her interest grew gradually.

It was a pleasant diversion and it passed the time, especially in the evening.

(As you no doubt know, in that early period of widowhood the evenings can be long. So. Very. Long.)

An example of the opposite is a story a woman in our group shared. Her husband had died about a year before and her friends were encouraging her to go hiking with them. (Yes, in the Northwest longtime hikers keep up that pastime well into their sixties and beyond.)

She kept turning them down. She had no interest in doing that anymore.

After the former-hiker, or hiker-on-hiatus, finished her story other men and women sitting around the table nodded in agreement. Similar things were happening to them.

Why? *Specifically*, why? Who knows? It could be none of them could answer that. There are so many unknowns, so many things that can't be explained, when your world is ripped apart.

I can't answer it. And it happened to me. I used to consider a social call on the telephone "long" if it lasted five minutes. That was the case even if I was out of town on work and was checking in with Monica back home.

Now—and this amuses my daughter who had been on the other end of those terse conversations—I spend hours each week visiting with family members (including my daughter), friends, and fellow widowhood "club members."

And I love it. Each conversation is a comfort, a joy, a delight.

I'm reminded of a quote from St. Paul: "When I was a child, I used to talk as a child, think as a child, reason as a child; when I became a man, I put aside childish things" (1 Corinthians 13:11). Only in this case it's: When I was married, I used to … . When I became widowed, I … .

That's not to say married-to-widowed is the same as child-to-adult. Obviously not. Still, there's a change. Or better put, a transition. That is, *a continuing change over a period of time.*

And part of it is putting aside some old things and

testing some new ones. It's *you* discovering what works, and what doesn't work, for *you*. It's *your* pathway on *your* pilgrimage.

There never has been, and never again will be, one just like it.

A little off topic here but I want to mention the two verses that directly follow St. Paul on a child and an adult, verses that conclude Chapter 13:

"At present we see indistinctly, as in a mirror [meaning a first-century, very primitive item], but then face to face. At present I know partially; then I shall know fully, as I am fully known. So faith, hope, love remain, these three; but the greatest of these is love."

At present you have an idea of what heaven, what the hereafter, is like for your dear one, but it's far from clear. But there will come a time, through the grace of God, when you'll know fully. A time when you and your loved one will be together again forever.

In the meantime, there's faith, hope, and love. And the greatest, the one that death didn't conquer, didn't stop, is love.

You still love your spouse. And your spouse still loves you.

Thank you, Lord, for letting some new things, some good things, seep into my new life.

39

MEMORIALS TO YOUR LOVED ONE

Monica and I share a headstone. Mine is still waiting for a year of death to be added.

(I've sometimes told people it reads "TBD" now: To Be Determined. A few believed me.)

That's one kind—probably the most common kind—of memorial a widow or widower gets for a spouse. But I've heard of other kinds, too. Often in addition to the headstone. And unlike the headstone which (usually) is put in place soon after a loved one's death, other memorials may come to mind, be considered, and be chosen or dismissed years after your spouse passes away.

One example is what my mom did five or six years after my dad died. His high school was making one of those fundraising "brick" pathways that would have names and dates of graduation on them. It pleased her to make a donation to have his name included.

Another example is a widow who found out a county park would install a picnic table or viewing-spot bench in memory of a loved one. This was about two years after her husband died. They had been big on hiking (and going mushroom hunting) and a bench or table could be placed in a park they loved and visited regularly over many years.

She talked about that at a support group meeting one time, asking for our opinions on whether she should choose a table or a bench. From stories she had previously told us, we knew that among her husband's varied and many talents, interests, and accomplishments, he had been an excellent cook and gracious host. We recommended the table.

She said she'd think about it.

A month or so later she sent me an email saying she was going with the picnic table and she could have a small plaque on it with his name, dates of birth and death, and a very short tribute. Knowing I was a writer, she asked for my help. I tweaked the suggested copy she sent me and then she finalized it to her deep, deep satisfaction.

It reads: "My Renaissance man who brought a zest for life to our table."

Later, she would visit the site and sit for a while at "their" table.

In your early grief, doing something like that probably won't occur to you. (It didn't for my friend. She had no idea the park did such things.) But farther down her path of widowhood, there it was. The same may end up being true for you, too. A challenge? Certainly. Causing more than a few tears? Absolutely. But… an act that can bring comfort and joy.

Because Monica and I were the cofounders of the Friends of St. John the Caregiver, I was familiar with those who are grieving making a donation to it in memory of a loved one. Most often, they do that because it had helped them care for that loved one.

As your pilgrimage continues there may be a time when you want to make a donation to an organization or cause that meant a lot to your loved one, to both of you, or to you alone. Perhaps to mark an anniversary or in place of the Christmas or birthday gift you would have given him or her if … things had turned out differently.

Dear Lord, I look forward to the day when happy memories of the two of us—my loved one and me—won't bring so many tears.

40
WIDOWHOOD IS ONE OF GOD'S "CURVE BALLS"

I think if God played Major League Baseball he'd be a pitcher. Mostly fastballs. (Life goes by so quickly!) And then, just to mix things up, an occasional curve ball.

A *big* curve ball.

I suspect that's how most people eligible for AARP membership (age 50 and up) would summarize their lives. The years blew by, and there were these amazing surprises. Out of the blue. Some were incredibly wonderful, others … so very far from that.

Good or bad, those were the curve balls.

But, unlike a baseball pitcher, God *wants* me to hit his fastball. And his curve.

To rewrite a verse from Zephaniah 3:17: "God takes great delight in me when I knock one out the park."

In my own life, I can see that the curves have included meeting Monica when we were twenty. Then a series of fast balls: falling in love, getting married, having kids and grandkids. And then another curve when we were sixty: her death from cancer.

It seemed that suddenly I was married (great surprise!)

and suddenly I wasn't married anymore (horrible surprise!).

Yes, love is stronger than death and I believe in the Communion of Saints, but in the eyes of the state and the Church, I'm now single. And like a young, just-wedded fellow figuring out married life so long ago, after her death I found myself a not-so-young, just-widowed fellow figuring out this new stage of my life.

(Forgive me for interrupting here but early in my widowhood I would joke that in the eyes of the state and the Church I was single, but I *still* had in-laws. How did *that* work? (Really, my in-laws were, and are, terrific.))

Decades ago I was shocked to discover my basic vocation (single, married, or religious life) was married. I really thought religious life, the priesthood, was going to be it.

But, it seems, God and Monica were in cahoots, and I'm so very grateful for that.

(And, no, I don't feel called to the priesthood now. Perhaps God has had time to think it over more carefully. Perhaps Monica has recently pointed out to him, face to face, why it still would be a bad idea.)

Like marriage, this singlehood subcategory—widowhood—takes adjusting to. Unlike marriage, the adjustments can be overwhelmingly unpleasant. To put it mildly.

Still … God's on the mound and he wants me to do something, something good, with the pitch he's just served up.

He wants me to do something good with the rest of my life, whether that lasts four days or forty-plus years.

I just don't get you, God. But, oh, how I need you.

41
NOW WHAT, LORD?

One widow I know said that soon after her husband died she felt her life had become a postscript. Just a little something added to what had been but now was no more.

I thought of mine as Act III. Monica and I met when we were twenty (end Act I) and she died when we were sixty (end Act II).

At sixty, I was fairly young for a widower. I still worked as a freelance writer and still wanted to be around for my kids because they, in their thirties, were pretty young to have lost a parent. And I wanted to be there for my grandkids—at ages seven and four—because … . Well, they were a delight.

I don't think it's uncommon for a widow or widower, especially one older than I had been, to begin to question "Why am I still here?"

And to fail to immediately find an even remotely satisfactory answer.

What you *want* is to be reunited with your spouse. In this life or the next. Why doesn't God just take care of that? In the early days, weeks, and months of widowhood—during that time of the "great blur"—existence on earth can be so very, very hard.

You know that. Deep in your bones. Your heart. Your soul.

That's not to say you want to end your own life. (And if you have those thoughts it's a strong indicator that you need to seek professional help. It truly *can* help.) It's just that your life, now led alone, can seem pointless.

You're "alone," even if there are many others still in your life. Including, for some widows and widowers, young children who need a parent's care. Now, more than ever, because their mom or dad—their mommy or daddy—has died.

In those instances, "now *what*?" may be more "now *how*?" "Now how do I do this as a single parent?" "How do I fill both parental roles?" "How do I give my children comfort in their grief when I'm so steeped in mine?" "How am I going to afford raising them?"

Whether in their twenties or their nineties, a widow or widower begins to adjust. Bit by bit, baby step by baby step. Each day, each night. Each week, each month. Each year. A little farther down this path that is their pilgrimage.

Your pilgrimage.

Now, always, you're heading toward that reunion with the one you love so deeply.

In big and little ways the "now what?" will be answered time and again. "I can do *this*." "It would be good if I did *that*." "I'm so glad I was able to do … ."

There'll be work to do, and blessings to be had, in this new and unchosen vocation.

Even so … .

As one young widow put it: "When I get to heaven, God's going to have a lot of explaining to do."

Now what, Lord? Break it to me gently.

42
REDEFINING "FINE"

My parents, sibling, and I froze our first "summer" in Seattle.

I had just finished sixth grade when my family left the Midwest for this strange new land of western Washington state. It never got really warm during the "summer" days. And the nights were always cold.

Then, too, there were the number of gray days versus the number of sunny days.

I don't remember the summer after seventh grade. By then, I assume, we had become acclimated. Seventy-five degrees was hot. Eighty-five was blistering. Late evening almost always meant a sweatshirt or jacket.

That was, simply, "summer." It has been for the past half century.

I thought about that recently when I realized I was tired of the ways I answered people's "How are you?"

After Monica died I fell into a pattern of answering "OK," "up and down," or "all right … all things considered." "Good" or "fine" never came to mind.

Yes, of course, things could have been worse, much worse, but my life seemed far from good. Far from fine.

As the months went by, I knew that for others, for those not close to Monica, her death was a long time ago. Six months. A year. Two years. It was some time in the vague past, they weren't quite sure when. If they asked, I'd tell them. If they guessed wrong, I would gently correct them.

"Two years? Wow." Then: "The time goes so fast." Or: "A long time now."

I would nod, but think: Those days and those nights didn't go fast for me. But, at times, it seems like only yesterday.

(One of widowhood's oxymorons (a figure of speech in which apparently contradictory terms appear in conjunction): "a recent long ago." Not as challenging as another: "completely numb but in incredible pain.")

Then, recently, something strange happened. Out of the blue, I thought, I'm tired of answering "OK" or "all right." I need to redefine "fine."

I thought: If I were in an accident and could no longer walk, when would I be "fine"? Would it be after ten years in a wheelchair? Twenty? If, two decades after that accident, someone asked, "How are you doing, Bill?" would I tell him, "How am I doing? I'm in a wheelchair, that's how I'm doing!"

After the death of a child or grandchild, when is a person "fine"?

After a divorce, when is a person "fine"?

After … after … after … .

Each of us is forced to face things we don't want to face. Learn things we don't want to learn. Experience things we don't want to experience. Live with things we don't want to live with. Things that change us forever. Things that never "go away."

It takes time to acclimate to our new life. It takes time for us to redefine "fine."

There are no timelines for that to happen. No countdowns. No circling a date on a calendar and thinking

"Oh, good, only this many more days and I'll . . . ."

It takes work. Patience. Perseverance. Prayer. And the grace of God.

But even then, sometimes we won't be doing fine. Triggered or "untriggered," those crushing emotions and memories will well up from the depths and dominate.

For a time. Just for a time.

Then, once again, we'll be fine.

I'm not asking to feel perfectly fine right now, Dear Lord.
I'll settle for "just a little better."

43
APPRECIATING RIGHT HERE, RIGHT NOW

"What time is it *really*?"

That's what our son, Thomas, wanted to know when Monica and I took our three young children (Thomas, Carrie, and Andy) on a road trip across the United States back in 1989.

Cross an invisible line and suddenly Mom and Dad adjust their wristwatches. Heading east, lose an hour. Heading west, gain one.

But what time is it *really*?

I remember when the kids were even younger and a snippet from Carly Simon's song *Anticipation* popped into my head one day and I realized it applied to me, to us. That later, looking back, these *were* going to be the good old days.

I had my doubts.

Three grade-schoolers running us ragged, a tight household budget, worries about work, an infinite to-do list, and on and on. Even so, at some point down the road, I'll consider right now "the good old days"? Ha!

And now I do, because they were.

In the blink of an eye, the children are grown. The house is quiet. My schedule is casual. My expenses minimal. My darling Monica … is gone. Taken by cancer.

I don't kid myself that way-back-when was a perfect time. There are no perfect times on earth although, thanks be to God, there can be near-perfect moments. Seen in the rear-view mirror of life, they sparkle and shine. They bring comfort and joy, even as they stand in stark contrast to change and loss.

Since Monica's death I've told myself "these, too, are the good old days." But that can't be, can it? Without her? Possibly for years, or decades?

They can be. They are.

I see the children often. The grandkids are wonderful. My parents have passed away but all my sibling are alive and well, and we laugh a lot when we get together. I have good friends. Good health. I have work I'm good at and want to continue doing as long as I can. I have … .

A good life. But not a perfect life. Good days. But not perfect days.

Like you, I have now. Right now. Like, you, I have here. Right here.

We have life on earth.

To use two popular modern terms, we're called to be present. To be mindful.

When I was about two years into widowhood, I realized I can't let myself become so obsessed thinking about a future without Monica that I fail to appreciate and use the blessings I have right here, right now. And I can't allow myself to become lost in, obsessed with, the past.

The truth is every age and every stage of a person's life has blessings and challenges. And with the passing of time and the grace of God, sometimes it's possible to see that the deepest blessings have their roots in the harshest challenges.

Sometimes it's possible to notice one constant through it all: Emmanuel, "God with us."

God with you.

Thank you for so many blessings, Dear God. Help me be better aware of your presence through so many challenges.

44
POCKETS OF GRIEF

I don't know at what point the scale tipped. When a day, and a night, were more not-grieving than grieving.

It wasn't like the changing seasons, with my knowing that by June the harshness of January weather would be long gone. That long, dark winter nights would give way to long, bright summer days.

I suppose I had to take it on faith that this grieving/not-grieving balance would shift. Faith in what a loss-and-grief social worker and veteran widows and widowers told me. Faith in a belief that God hadn't abandoned me and wouldn't leave me forever in this life—this pit—where I was living now.

It was reassuring when I saw that those of us who were recently widowed were going through those early times not only in our own individual ways but at our own pace. The ways that were working best for us and the pace that was … the pace. My ways. My pace. My pilgrimage.

My grief.

Since then, the weeks, months, and years have helped me learn to anticipate and prepare myself for yearly events (birthdays, anniversaries, and such) and the big events (a birth, a death, and so on) that are the part of every person's life.

I know that there can be "triggers." A song on the radio. A sudden thought that "Oh, I'll have to tell Monica about … ." A sight. A smell. A memory.

But it's only recently that I started thinking about my sudden and unexpected "falling into grief" as "pockets of grief." That I started noticing that it seems I'm gliding along OK and then, like an airplane sailing through clear skies that unexpectedly hits an air pocket, I drop emotionally.

It's startling.

What happened? Why did it happen? Now what?

I've noticed the pocket doesn't last long. It's not crashing or crushing. It's not entering an extended period of turbulence. It's a morning, a day, a couple of days, where I just feel sad again. Not the grief of those early times, not the sorrow that's so debilitating, but … just sad. Just missing Monica. Just once again feeling more focused on her not being here and what a crummy thing that is.

I make it through. In this analogy, the plane returns to its standard operating altitude and levels off. The pilot turns off the fasten-seatbelt sign and, once again, I'm free to move about the cabin. But the captain gets on the intercom to advise it's best to have that seatbelt loosely fastened even when the sign is off.

It's best for me to do the same as a widower, even during an extended period of smooth flying.

To get enough sleep. To eat wisely. To exercise. To stay pleasantly busy. To pray for others and their needs.

An airplane seatbelt doesn't somehow prevent air pockets but I suspect paying attention to my needs, to my own well-being, does make those sudden, startling emotional drops less severe, more manageable, and briefer.

Dear Lord, when I hit a "grief pocket," help me remember it's only temporary and that I'm going to be OK.

45
SOMEWHERE *INSIDE* THE RAINBOW

At some point after Monica died, perhaps it had been nine or ten months, I realized I was a "longtime widower" in the eyes of those whose spouse had died only a few weeks or a month or two ago.

I was able to help them in some small ways because my baby steps had moved me along my path. Along my pilgrimage. I hadn't gotten far, but at the same time, I'd gone *some* distance.

And those recently widowed men and women helped me. I saw that I was no longer where they were right then. (Although, of course, there were times when I went back to an earlier point. That still happens.) Now I know that without them trusting me and talking to me I wouldn't have been aware I had been going forward and wouldn't have appreciated the (small) progress I'd made.

It wasn't crossing a sharp and obvious line, like Monica's dying had been. It was more like an overwhelming red gradually and subtly becoming more orange. And, as the years have gone by, perhaps my own pilgrimage could be described as continuing on through a spectrum of colors. Reaching a warm yellow, with a lessening of fear and anxiety. To a green, the symbol of hope and some new life in my "new life."

Then, blue. Then, calm. Then, peace.

Even now I slide from color to color. (Maybe a bit like the old board game of Chutes and Ladders!) Back to red, To orange. To yellow. To green. And so, again, I start my way through that spectrum from that point. It's easier now. It takes less time. It's a path that's not unfamiliar to me.

I realize this is far from a perfect analogy. (Doesn't everyone recently widowed feel "blue," meaning down and depressed? And doesn't a prism's spectrum include indigo and purple?) And your experiences might be different from mine. Most likely *are* different from mine because yours are yours alone. And the same is true for me and mine.

For every widow and widower.

For *each* widow and widower.

But … .

Based on what I've seen among the widows and widowers in "my class" over the past five years—the ones I've known since all of us were puddles of tears—I will say this:

Calm comes.

Peace is possible.

For you.

Dearest Mother Mary, Our Lady in Blue, pray for me.

46

GIFTS FROM A HOLE SO DEEP

One of the early images I had for my grief was losing a tooth. A big one. A molar. There was this hole and I wanted to be rid of it. But I knew I couldn't fill it by just … filling it. Like a new tooth replacing an old, something would—with time—grow into it. I just didn't know what that would be. Or how long it would take.

Another image was a deep, deep hole inside of me. Time and again I would fall into it. Sometimes first thing in the morning—or in the middle of the night—I would wake up there. Often I would stumble into it during the day.

I remember when I was out on a walk in the neighborhood I would tell myself to just stop thinking about Monica dying and me being alone. Think about something else for a few minutes. But it took only a step or two and I was back to it. Like some kind of a towering wall about a foot in front of me. No way around it. Or over it, under it, or through it.

Wherever I went, whatever I did, there it was. Right there. In my face. On my mind, in my heart, filling my soul.

You may have other ways of describing what's happening to you. And those ways may change with time.

One no longer fits, but another seems accurate.

Now, four years later, when I think about those walks with that wall in front of me wherever I turned, I realize I did go through it. Not ramming it. Not smashing it to pieces. But, in so many ways throughout each of those days, by "putting one foot in front of the other."

Sometimes that meant pushing myself a little. When I could. Sometimes it meant giving myself a break. Even when it bothered me that I needed to take (another!) break and I would have preferred to be able to do this or that.

("What's wrong with me?" I'd say to myself. "All I need to do is … ." Work a little on something that should be done around the house. Agree to go out to lunch with a family member or friend. Get some writing work done for an upcoming deadline.)

Looking back, I can see I was taking "baby steps." So tiny. So teetering. So unsure. And while I was doing that, the hole inside me was filling. It was, and is, still there but not as deep. Not as all-consuming. And from it have come two gifts for which I'm so grateful.

Number one is a firsthand knowledge of what it means to become, and to be, widowed. It's not something I wanted but it's something I gained.

It's not something you wanted. It's something that you're gaining, too. And will continue to do so.

What that has come to mean for me is an ability to step right up and speak kindly with someone who is recently widowed. To say a few words about my own experience. To ask a few questions about theirs. To very informally invite them, a new "club member," to talk about their spouse. Their loss. Their "life" now.

And the second gift that horrible hole produced is strength. It comes with a strange feeling of pride. *I* did that. My wife died and I did all those things that are a part of early widowhood and here I am.

Still here. I am.

I want to be clear on this. I'm not saying I was strong as a new widower. I'm saying that by going through those early days, weeks, months, and years of widowhood I've become strong. By taking those baby steps.

Now, when I need to face some difficult or challenging situation (including those that are widowhood-related), I'm inclined to say, "I did *that.*" (Meaning made it through early widowhood.) "I can do *this.*" (Whatever it may be.)

That's been my experience. Yours will be yours. But, I think, the God-given gifts that await you are like the gold that was tested in fire (1 Pt 1:7). They're gifts, they're hard-earned treasures, that are yours to use for the benefit of others and for yourself as you continue to baby-step forward in your new vocation of widowhood.

On your path. Your pilgrimage.

Dear Lord, give me a few minutes of peace. A time when I'm not anxious, sad, frightened, or tired. And let those times come more frequently and last longer.

APPENDIX 1

WIDOW AND WIDOWER PRAYERS

(from the end of each chapter)

1

Dear Lord, I'm overwhelmed. I'm terrified. I'm lost.
Dear, Dear Lord, be with me right here, right now.

2

Thank you, Dear Lord, for sparing my dear __________ from having to endure widowhood. Thank you for letting me be the one to take the hit.

3

Gently lead me, Lord. Patiently guide me.

4

I don't need to know all the answers, Lord,
but please ease my pain.

5

Widow Mary, Our Lady of Sorrows,
pray for me, pray with me.

6

Dearest Lord, please give me a moment of peace today.

7

Out of the depths of grief I cry to you, Lord;
Lord, hear my prayer!

8

Holy Spirit, Great Comforter and Consoler,
help me sleep better.

9

Dear Holy Spirit, give me the wisdom to find my path
on this pilgrimage and to make my way forward.

10

Thank you, Lord, that I'm learning more about living with
my loss and my grief so I can better live with my loss
and my grief. I just wish these lessons weren't so hard.
Sometimes, so brutal.

11

Thank you, Dear Lord, for the "gift" of tears.
(And for vigorous nose-blowing, too.)

12

Today, Dear Lord, I pray for those
who are just beginning their widowhood.

13

Thank you, Lord, for my dear, dear ________________. I
can't count all the ways I love him/her.

14

Help me pay attention, Lord,
when you tell me to sit down. To just stop.

Help me rest.

15

Dear Jesus, help me accept and do my Heavenly Father's
will even when I hate what he's asking of me.

16

When I'm ready and able, Lord,
help me accept more help from others.

17

Dear Lord, the story of my life includes
such a devastating loss.
Be with me now.

18

Dear Lord, help me find people I can talk to about all this,
and help me hear what they're saying.

19

Holy Spirit, help those who are grieving find the support
they need. (Including me!)

20

Heavenly Father, give me the strength
to find and use the help I need.

21

Please, Lord, help me not feel guilty
when there are things I want to do but just can't.
Not right now. Not yet.

22

Heavenly Father, help me find the ways to find my way.

23

Just for now, Holy Spirit, ease my pain.
Bring me a moment of peace.

24

Heavenly Father, protect me from those who mean well but don't know what they're talking about, or who are just bossy, and give me the strength to make it through today.

25

Holy Spirit, give me the wisdom to make good decisions and to trust myself more.

26

Prince of (Inner) Peace, be with me now.

27

Walk with me, Dear Jesus, as I stumble and bumble through this time. Help me hang on to you.

28

Thank you, Dear Lord, for the ability to ask for forgiveness, to forgive, and to accept forgiveness. And thank you for the sacrament of reconciliation.

29

Thank you, Lord, for moments of happiness. Help me see each one as a gift from my dear ______________,
as something sent special delivery …
and sealed with a kiss.

30

Dear Lord, forgive me for what I have done and what I have failed to do. Dear Lord, help me forgive myself.

31
Heavenly Father, help me rest. Help me sleep. Help me.

32
Oh, Dear Holy Spirit, how I dread some upcoming birthdays, anniversaries, and holidays. Be with me, be with me, be with me.

33
Dear Lord, help me take care of myself, especially when I'm afraid to do that.

34
Heavenly Father, help me mark this Lent with the gentle and loving ways you're calling me to do that. Help me avoid getting caught up in my own ideas of what "I should" be doing over these forty days.

35
Holy Spirit, help me work on my grief in the ways and at the pace that are best for me.

36
Lord, help the friendships that are important to me continue and grow deeper. And maybe let me make some new, dear friends, too.

37
I'm glad you never change, God. I love you just the way you are. (Even if you can be so hard to understand!)

38
Thank you, Lord, for letting some new things, some good things, seep into my new life.

39

Dear Lord, I look forward to the day when happy memories of the two of us—my loved one and me—won't bring so many tears.

40

I just don't get you, God. But, oh, how I need you.

41

Now what, Lord? Break it to me gently.

42

I'm not asking to feel perfectly fine right now, Dear Lord. I'll settle for "just a little better."

43

Thank you for so many blessings, Dear God. Help me be better aware of your presence through so many challenges.

44

Dear Lord, when I hit a "grief pocket," help me remember it's only temporary and that I'm going to be OK.

45

Dearest Mother Mary, Our Lady in Blue, pray for me.

46

Dear Lord, give me a few minutes of peace. A time when I'm not anxious, sad, frightened, or tired. And let those times come more frequently and last longer.

APPENDIX 2
TIPS ON FINDING A SUPPORT GROUP

Chapter 19 focused on "Finding Formal and Informal Support" and, as promised, this appendix offers tips on finding a group to help you.

It could be at this point in your widowhood—whether it's weeks, months or years after the death of your loved one—there's an increased feeling of needing some kind of support. But you aren't sure what, where, who, or even why.

Why now and not earlier? Because your grief is unique. Some need the help of a support group earlier, some later. Some, not at all.

Again, just as your relationship and marriage were one-of-a-kind, so too with your grief and what's best for your handling it … as you're manhandled by it.

Not so much conquering it as coming to terms with it. Not, in some way, slaying it but learning to live with it.

That being said, here are some suggestions for finding the right support group or series of classes on grief.

- Ask family, friends, and fellow parishioners if they attended (or still attend) a support group after the death of a loved one. Find out where it met and who sponsored it.

- If searching for a group seems too much—if not impossible—right now, ask someone you trust to do a little research for you. Let them call around and hunt on the web and share what they find.
- Your parish or another parish in your area may have a bereavement ministry that includes a support group. So, too, with the diocese and other faith communities.
- Hospitals and medical centers may sponsor a group. Health maintenance organizations (HMOs) and medical insurance providers may have support groups open to all, not just members.
- The same is true for hospice and palliative care providers. (Perhaps including the one that helped your spouse and you.)
- Some funeral homes have support groups. Call them or look online at their websites. If they don't, they might know of one that does.
- A local cemetery association (including your diocese's) may have one or know of some. (Your local Catholic cemetery may also have a monthly Mass onsite for those who have lost a loved one.)
- Your employer may have a group or can recommend one. Check with HR.
- A place to start a localized web search can be "grief support" or "bereavement support" followed with the name of your town, city, or county.

APPENDIX 3

A HANDOUT SHEET TO SHARE WITH FAMILY AND FRIENDS

Available in a printable format at billdodds.com/I_Would_Like_You_to_Know.pdf

"A FEW THINGS I WOULD LIKE YOU TO KNOW ABOUT WIDOWHOOD"

1. I don't talk about what's really going on because you probably think, just as I thought, that after six months, a year, ten or more years, I should be "over it." Or that I am over it. Time doesn't completely heal all wounds. The grief of becoming a widow or widower diminishes but it's like a chronic condition that I learn to live with, knowing it can flare up at any time.

2. I know it's hard for you to say "the right thing" when you see me for the first time after my spouse died. But please don't tell me you know *exactly* how I feel. (Please don't mention you had a cat that died!) There is no one-size-fits-all "right thing." In fact, it's comforting when you admit, "I don't know what to say." Tell me you're sorry they died.

Tell me they and I are in your prayers. Tell me a story about them. Something wonderful or funny you remember.

3. Don't be afraid to talk about my dear one just because that makes me cry. It's so much worse to have no one say their name. To have so many family members and friends act as if they never existed. My crying doesn't bother me. I've become a world-class crier. I'm not offended or upset if you send an email or call me on their birthday or our wedding anniversary or the date of their death. I love that! Love it, love it, love it!

4. Now my happiest moments can also have a sad undertone to them. My son is graduating from college! My daughter is getting married! I have my first grandchild! And this is happening … without my beloved spouse by my side. It was supposed to be "us" celebrating this event. And it's "me." Only "me." It helps to know you're aware of their absence, too. If we reminisce a little about them.

5. I'm not the same person I was before they died. I live on the same planet but it's a different world without them. This huge loss is made up of countless small losses that are a part of my days. And nights.

6. You can help, and you do help, by graciously inviting me to gatherings even if I continue to say "no thanks." By your understanding if, at the last minute, I call to say I can't come. By being patient if, when I'm there, I'm distracted sometimes. Even in the middle of a crowd of loved ones, sometimes I'm lonely because, in a very basic way, I *am* there alone. But your ongoing support and understanding and prayers mean a great deal to me. They continue to make a huge difference as I stumble along. And I'm so very grateful for them. And you.

ABOUT THE AUTHOR

Bill Dodds is an award-winning and best-selling author. He's had more than three dozen books published, including fiction and non-fiction for adults and children. One year after the death of his wife, Monica, in 2013, he wrote the novel *Mildred Nudge: A Widower's Tale.*

In 2005, Monica and Bill founded the Friends of St. John the Caregiver, an international Catholic organization that promotes care for family caregivers (www.FSJC.org).

For more information about Bill and his work visit www.BillDodds.com. He can be reached at WFDodds@gmail.com.

Made in the
USA
Lexington, KY